MW00474522

A PLAY IN TWO ACTS

By N. Richard Nash

S A M U E L F R E N C H, I N C.
45 West 25th Street   NEW YORK, N.Y. 10010
7623 Sunset Boulevard   HOLLYWOOD 90046
LONDON   *TORONTO*

A young man and woman build a paradise of happiness within an asylum, only to have it shattered by the intrusion of the outside world. How this happens is made into an absorbing drama by N. Richard Nash.

The two characters search, at times agonizingly, to determine the difference between illusion and reality. The effort is lightened at times by moments of shared love and "pretend" games, but it is basically a deeply serious play. The theme of love, vulnerable to the surveillances of The Place, and the ministrations of The Person, a non-speaking part (because the pair cannot—or won't—hear him?) seems as fragile in the constrained setting as it often is in the outside world.

ECHOES is not an easy play, but even with the tragic theme there is a note of hope and possible release and the situations presented specifically also have universal applications to give it a powerful effect. It is intellectual, but charged with emotion.

ECHOES WAS THE 1972 AWARD PLAY OF *THE AMERICAN PLAYWRIGHTS THEATRE*, THE ASSOCIATION OF OVER 200 UNIVERSITY AND COMMUNITY THEATRES.

ECHOES was presented at A Contemporary Theatre in Seattle, Washington on August 8, 1972. The play was directed by Gregory A. Falls; the setting was by S. Todd Muffati and the lighting by Phil Schermer. The cast was as follows:

TILDA .... *Gisela Caldwell*

SAM .... *Stanley Anderson*

THE PERSON .... *Ben Tone*

ECHOES was presented in New York City at the Bijou Theatre on March 26, 1973. The play was produced by Orin Lehman and directed by Melvin Bernhardt; the setting was by Ed Wittstein, the lighting by Martin Aronstein and the costumes by Sara Brook. The cast was as follows:

TILDA .... *Lynn Milgrim*

SAM .... *David Selby*

THE PERSON .... *Paul Tripp*

Echoes

ACT ONE

THE PLACE *is bare except for a seemingly haphazard arrangment of wooden boxes. Nearly all of them are hexahedron in shape—cubes, for the most part, with a few that are rectangular. One or two are squat cylinders. They are painted in various warm colors, not too bright, muted and somewhat worn.*

THE PLACE *is dark. When the lights come on—in the gradual suffusion of a warm morning—we see* SAM *and* TILDA *asleep, not far from each other.* TILDA *is the first to awaken, with languid felicity. Because she is an inmate of The Place one must not think of her as an unhappy girl. On the contrary, she has found her own springs of joy. For a moment, as always happens when* TILDA *awakens, she has no notion where to find herself. Gradually her perceptions clear and she sees something . . . that isn't there. A window. Slowly, in an animus difficult to identify—a cold resentment, awe perhaps—she advances to the imaginary plate of glass and looks through it. She cannot see anything except reflections. They bother her. She puts her hands up, both palms against the glass surface as if to measure its size, texture, vulnerability, its very existence. Now she makes a fist and tentatively raps on the nonexistent window; pounds on it, it doesn't break; her face is terrified for one instant. Relief comes when she hears a sound. We hear it too. It's a snore. She turns quickly and sees* SAM. *Her mood, as she watches him sleep, slowly changes, brightens like*

5

sunrise. The sight of him enraptures her. She starts to awaken him.

TILDA. Sam! . . . Sammy! . . . Sa-mu-el! (*As he stirs but doesn't awaken.*) Sammy—please—wake up!

SAM. What? . . . What? (*He comes partially awake. He is somewhat older than* TILDA—*perhaps eight or ten years older. He is no brighter than she but has learned more. His humor is not so ready as hers, but goes deeper.*)

TILDA. Wake up, Sammy! (*Unexpectedly—play-acting —he jumps up, fully awake.*)

SAM. What? What's happening? Did I miss something?

TILDA. (*Delighted by him.*) Oh, I love the way you wake up!

SAM. What? What did I miss? What's happening?— where did you go?

TILDA. One minute you're dead asleep—and the next minute you're in a parade!

SAM. (*Showing off.*) What's up? When did you get here?

TILDA. I've been here all the time!—waiting for you to stop snoring and get up!

SAM. I didn't snore!—did I?

TILDA. You went chluch-chluch a few times and once you whistled.

SAM. Off-key, I bet!

TILDA. (*She points.*) . . . Look, Sammy. (*The spot she is indicating, in an island surrounded by boxes, is empty. Not to them.* SAM *sees what she is pointing to— and is overcome with the beauty of it.*)

SAM. It's still there!

TILDA. Of course it's still there.

SAM. It's beautiful, isn't it?

TILDA. Yes. And the branches have settled a little.

SAM. I told you they would. You think it's too tall?

TILDA. No, I love a tall tree. Oh, Sammy, it's the prettiest tree I've ever seen in my whole life.

SAM. That's what you're supposed to say every year.

If you say anything short of that, it's ugly. (*In action.*) All right, let's decorate it.

TILDA. Wait!—do we have to? I love it the way it is!

SAM. Now, Tilda—we decided. (*Then, to soften her disappointment.*) You'll like it even better with the decorations—I promise you will! We'll have long strands of silver tinsel—and little candles—and Christmas canes —and lights! A thousand lights, Tilda! It'll be so bright you'll see it with your eyes closed!

TILDA. (*Smiling.*) I can do that now.

SAM. Come on. You want to put the icicles on?

TILDA. (*Outraged, she is pretending.*) Icicles? I despise icicles! They clutter up a tree! They vulgarize it! They're a cheap way of getting an ostentatious display, without the exercise of any taste or intelligence! Anybody who puts icicles on a Christmas tree is an enemy of decency!

SAM. I like your cool judicious view of the matter . . . Will we put an angel on the top?

TILDA. Why, of course! If I can climb up and put it on.

SAM. You'll fall.

TILDA. I won't—why should I fall?

SAM. All right, but I think we better untangle the lights first.

TILDA. Here's one that's all neat.

SAM. It's got a short in it.

TILDA. I'll plug it in and see. (*She starts to plug the imaginary strand of lights into the imaginary receptacle. He hurries to prevent her.*)

SAM. Careful, you'll get a shock! (*Too late—she has plugged it in.*)

TILDA. There—no shock. And every bulb lights up— every single bulb! (*She starts to jump rope with the imaginary strand of Christmas tree lights.*) Mabel, Mabel, set the table—don't forget the salt, vinegar, mustard, *pepper!*

SAM. Hey—quit that—you'll break the bulbs!

TILDA. (*As fast as she can.*) Pepper—pepper—pepper —pepper!

SAM. Stop it! (*She at last obeys. She is laughing and triumphant.*) Well, that's fine!—you broke five bulbs!

TILDA. I didn't! Not that many!

SAM. (*Ready to make a deal.*) How many?

TILDA. Three?

SAM. I'll settle for four. Now let's get it up on the tree.

TILDA. Shouldn't I put the angel up first?

SAM. Yes, where is it?

TILDA. Uh . . . would you trust me to make it?

SAM. Make an angel? From scratch?

TILDA. *Somebody* makes them from scratch.

SAM. All right. I'll put the lights up—you make the angel. (*He piles some boxes on top of each other and mounts them to string the lights on the tree. Meanwhile* TILDA *is debating with herself.*)

TILDA. Shall I do it with paste or shall I do it with thread? Thread! No—paste. Nah, I think I better do it with thread. (*She gets her imaginary materials together —paper, scissors, needles—and starts making the angel. She is deeply happy doing it and starts to hum. The song is "Take Me Out to the Ball Game."*)

SAM. What's that you're humming?

TILDA. A Christmas carol. (*As she continues humming, he listens doubtfully. Now she sings the words:*)
Take me out to the ball game,
Take me out with the crowd . . .

SAM. Are you sure that's a Christmas carol?

TILDA. (*No doubt of it.*) Oh yes. (*He debates whether to pursue the point but then doesn't.* TILDA *quits singing because of difficulty with the angel. She is now sewing parts of it together. She bites off a thread and daintily spits out the bit of it. Something's wrong with the angel. She starts talking to herself.*) Damn you, Tilda, I thought I told you not to do it with thread—I told you the stitches would break! Paste! I told you to use paste! It's used on everything nowadays! When a great big building starts to crack up what do they stick it together with? They use it on everything—broken knee-caps and broken promises and I knew a married couple, they were splitting up and how do you think they got themselves stuck together again?

SAM. (*Interrupting.*) You're talking to yourself.

TILDA. Yes I am. And if it was myself I was talking to, it was very rude of you to butt into the conversation.

SAM. I don't like it when you talk to yourself.

TILDA. Don't you ever talk to yourself?

SAM. (*Annoyed.*) No, I don't—I don't find it very interesting.

TILDA. Then one of you must be a bore . . . maybe both.

SAM. (*Testily.*) I don't talk to myself *out loud!*

TILDA. What's the difference between talking to yourself silently and talking to yourself out loud?

SAM. Well, if you don't see the difference—! (*Exploding.*) It's an insult, that's the difference!

TILDA. An insult? To whom?

SAM. Me!

TILDA. How?

SAM. Well, if you've got me to talk to and you don't—

TILDA. (*Interrupting.*) There are some things I don't want to talk to you about!

SAM. Then don't say them so I can hear them!

TILDA. You're not meant to hear them—you're eavesdropping!

SAM. (*Exasperated.*) Oh brother!—if you don't want me to *hear* you—

TILDA. I just don't understand! People make all that fuss about talking to yourself, but it's okay to sing to yourself. Not just humming—singing—with words! And sometimes they're the most ridiculous words! But that's okay—you can say the most asinine things as long as you sing 'em! Out loud—so the whole world can hear! But the minute you talk to yourself—just plain talk—bang!—you're in here!

SAM. (*Quietly.*) That's not the only reason you're in here.

TILDA. (*An instant. Then, also quiet.*) . . . No . . . Wouldn't it be nice if that were the only reason? . . . (*She thinks about this quite soberly, then goes back to sewing her angel.*)

SAM. I got the whole strand of lights on. Shall we try it?

TILDA. Sure—let's.

SAM. I'll shove the plug in. (*He comes down from the tree, follows the wire, gets to the electrical outlet.*) Well, here we go. (*He shoves the plug in, gets a shock, screams.*) Ow!—Christ!—ow!—ow!

TILDA. What?—what?

SAM. What-do-you-think-what? I told you that lousy thing had a short!

TILDA. It didn't for me! It worked!

SAM. It's working all right, but it's got a short in it!

TILDA. (*Swooning with delight as she sees the lights.*) Oh, look how beautiful it is!

SAM. Who cares about beautiful? I'll never have the use of my right arm again!

TILDA. Stop being a cry-baby—look! (*He stops being in pain. He turns to look at the tree. He is as overcome with its beauty as she is.*) Let's not do any more to it. We'll just spoil it.

SAM. That's what you said before we put the lights on.

TILDA. But there's a limit to how beautiful it can get.

SAM. (*Quietly.*) There's no limit to how beautiful we feel about it.

TILDA. . . . But there is, really.

SAM. Not in here there isn't.

TILDA. (*After a moment.*) Doesn't that scare you?

SAM. What?

TILDA. That there aren't any limits?

SAM. Why should it scare me that there's no end to beauty?

TILDA. Because then there's no end to all the rest. (*Silence. He stares at her. His gaze tenses. There is alarm in it.*)

SAM. Why did you call me that?

TILDA. Call you what?

SAM. You called me a strange name.

TILDA. A strange . . . ? (*Puzzled.*) I didn't call you anything. If I did, it was Sammy!

SAM. (*More perturbed.*) You called me something else! (*His hand suddenly going to his ear.*) It's gone now— I can't hear it any more! What was the name?

TILDA. Sammy, please—stop trying to remember.

SAM. I'm not trying to remember anything! I distinctly heard you call me a name I didn't recognize! Now, you tell me what it was!

TILDA. Sammy—

SAM. (*Getting angry.*) What was the name? What are you trying to do? Why are you lying to me?

TILDA. I'm not lying! If you heard anybody call you any other name than Sammy, you better blame somebody else!

SAM. There are only two of us!—who the hell can I blame?! I don't know his name any better than I know my own. (*Silence. Slowly, almost furtively,* TILDA'S *eyes go to the window.* SAM'S *eyes follow. At last they look away. Silence. Then:*)

TILDA. I wish we didn't have any fixed names.

SAM. You mean have a different one whenever we want it?

TILDA. Yes, a new one every morning! Then I'd wake up and wouldn't be responsible to somebody named Tilda, whoever that girl was last night! It's a damn nuisance having to answer to some stranger named Tilda who died yesterday! And having to answer to her tomorrow, before she's ever born! And when I think I'm going to have to answer to her next week and next year and all the mornings of my life—! (*She shudders, overdramatizing it.*)

SAM. (*With a half-hidden smile.*) But someday you might want to answer to her. She might be somebody you'd like . . . a friend.

TILDA. No, I can't imagine it—I don't think it's possible. Let's not talk about it. Let's play something.

SAM. Okay—play what?

TILDA. Let's play that you're a—a teacher!

SAM. (*Pause. Then:*) I *am* a teacher.

TILDA. (*Pretending to be delightfully surprised.*) Oh, what a coincidence! How smart of me to guess it!

SAM. (*His annoyance sharpening.*) Stop that!

TILDA. I didn't know that—honest I didn't!

SAM. Yes you did! I told you I was a teacher the first time we met! You've always known it! You knew it yesterday! And I told you then—

TILDA. (*Placating.*) All right—all right—

SAM.—I don't want to play that game!

TILDA. (*Also getting annoyed.*) I'm sorry, I'm sorry!

SAM. You're not sorry—you're just trying to sneak things around—

TILDA. I don't sneak!

SAM.—so that we can play real! (*Silence. It is a confrontation. She is unnerved by it, but at last, equal to it. She speaks with the utmost quiet.*)

TILDA. I don't want to play real—and you know it! I never want to play real. If I do it, it's because I think you prefer it that way.

SAM. (*Also quiet.*) Well, I don't.

TILDA. (*To change the mood.*) If you only had one wish—any wish in the world—what would you ask for?

SAM. I hate it when somebody gives me only one wish. It's like snatching away all the other ones. Suppose you had only one—what would you ask for?

TILDA. I'd wish that I . . . could break the window.

SAM. (*Gently.*) Tilda . . . please . . . let it alone.

TILDA. (*With quiet intensity.*) It's a terrible window!

SAM. Forget about it.

TILDA. I can't forget about it! What's the good of it? I can't see *through* the glass—and what I see *in* it—! (*She shudders.*)

SAM. Now come on, *what* do you see in it?

TILDA. (*Angry.*) Reflections of myself! And it's disgusting to see what I look like!

SAM. Then don't look there—look at me—I'll tell you what you look like.

TILDA. . . . What do *you* see in it, Sammy?

SAM. Never mind.

TILDA. Please tell me.

SAM. It's not what I see *now* . . .

TILDA. What do you hope to see?

SAM. (*Reluctant.*) You know as well as I do. Who I was before . . . and the people I knew. (*A moment, then.*) And . . . why.

TILDA. Why what?

SAM. Why everything.

TILDA. Who's ever going to see that in a window?

SAM. Nobody . . . That doesn't keep me from looking.

TILDA. (*A sudden desperation.*) I don't want to look! I don't want you to do it either! I hate that window! Some day you'll see right through it—and then you'll be gone!

SAM. Perhaps.

TILDA. I hate it! I'm going to break it! (*She rushes across the stage to break the window. She has her arm raised like a sledgehammer. SAM runs across to stop her.*)

SAM. Wait! No—stop!—wait!

TILDA. Break it! I'm going to break it!

SAM. I said stop it! (*He finally succeeds in stopping her, in calming her down. In rage.*) Don't you ever do that again! (*Now he controls himself. His voice resumes its customary gentleness.*) Please don't do that any more, honey. (*Trying to treat it with lightness.*) You break it and it'll be that much easier for me, won't it? I'll just walk right through it—and never come back.

TILDA. (*Appalled.*) . . . Never come back? (*A tense silence, then:*) Oh, I can't stand that—let's play baseball!

SAM. Do we have to?

TILDA. Yes, we have to!—come on!

SAM. (*A slow smile.*) I see. You don't want to break

the window—not on purpose. You just want to hit the ball so it goes through the glass—accidentally.

TILDA. (*Shocked.*) You think I would do that?—after what you just told me?

SAM. I said accidentally.

TILDA. Answer yes or no!

SAM. Yes *and* no—that's what an accident *is*.

TILDA. Holy mackerel, I just want to play baseball!

SAM. . . . All right. Who's at bat?

TILDA. I am.

SAM. I thought so.

TILDA. Now don't be snide, Sammy. You think if I'm at bat, I'll hit the ball right through the glass?—bang!— well, you're wrong! And to prove you're wrong, *you're* at bat! I'm pitching.

SAM. (*Surprised.*) Well, that's very nice of you.

TILDA. Pla-hay ba-hall!

SAM. Are you going to pitch or are you going to be the umpire?

TILDA. Both.

SAM. (*Suspiciously.*) Both?

TILDA. (*With lofty dignity.*) It may not have occurred to you that we're engaged in this enterprise with a short-age of personnel. If some of us are willing to do more than one job, others shouldn't be ungrateful.

SAM. Okay, pitch it.

TILDA. (*The umpire again.*) Batter u-hup!

SAM. The batter *is* up. Pitch it. (*She winds up elaborately like the most seasoned of pitchers. She whams it in. He jumps back as if it was so close to his body as to be dangerous.*) Jesus Christ!

TILDA. It wasn't even near you!

SAM. Wasn't near me? It knocked one of my buttons of!

TILDA. (*As the umpire.*) Strike one!

SAM. (*Apoplectic.*) Strike?—did you call that a strike?

Didn't you see me jump for my life?—you call that a strike?

TILDA. (*As the umpire.*) Pla-hay ball!

SAM. Instead of trying to get it over the plate, why don't you just aim it right at me! Right here—at my head! (*She has wound up. The pitch!*)

TILDA. (*The umpire.*) Strike Tee-oo!

SAM. (*With elaborate aggrievement.*) Okay—fine. Just fine! You keep throwing those close ones and call them all strikes and I'll be *out!*—one, two, three—and the game'll be over! Fine! I don't want to play baseball anyway!

TILDA. You know what?—you're a bad loser!

SAM. (*Affronted.*) Oh, I'm a loser, am I? The game just started and you've got me down as a loser!

TILDA. Well, you lost last time and it looks like I'm going to murder you this time!

SAM. (*With grandiloquent dignity.*) Okay—I'm murdered! Go no further! I—am—murdered! Game's over! (*He throws down his bat and quits.*)

TILDA. Come back here! You're a sorehead, a sorehead!

SAM. Right!—a sorehead!—absolutely right! I am a sorehead and a loser! And murdered—don't forget that! I'm a corpse!—therefore not perfectly suited to play ball with! If you've got any more names to call me, you just call them! How about thief?—that's what you called me last time! Or sneak!—that's a good name—how about sneak?

TILDA. Or creep!

SAM. Yes—oh yes! I like that!—creep!—you just call me that! That'll endear you to me—a lot! It'll make the game a thousand times more pleasant so that the next time you want to play I'll be so eager, I'll be so excited to play, I'll be so anxious to get that goddamn bat in my hands—! (*She starts to laugh. He stops his harangue. Suddenly he laughs too and they howl with the enjoyment of each other.*)

TILDA. Pla-hay ba-hall!

SAM. Pla-hay ba-hall!

SAM and TILDA. (*Together, shouting.*) Play ball, play ball, play ball!

SAM. (*At bat again—challenging, boasting.*) Now, come on, pitch it in there! And watch me get a hit! Watch me zing this right out over left field—way out there—over the fence and over the horizon and way out into the beautiful nowhere, the big blue beautiful nowhere! (*As he has been swinging his bat at the forthcoming pitch she has been studying him. Now she winds up. A slow, slow wind up. This is going to be a wicked one, she tells herself, a strike to strike him out. She lets it go. Bang!—he gets it in the eye.*) Ow! My eye! Oh!—ow!—oh, oh, oh! Jesus!—oh, Christ!—oh, I'm going to lose an eye!—oh murder, somebody call a doctor, call an ambulance! Oh, Jesus, I'll be walking around with an eye patch! Oh, I'm going to lose an eye! (*While he has been playing this aria, she has been trying to get to him, to pull his hands away from his face, to grab him, to make him sit down. She is beside herself with remorse and terror for the imaginary loss of his eye.*)

TILDA. (*Talking simultaneously with him.*) Oh, honey —oh, darling—let me see it! Oh, I'm sorry, darling— I'm sorry! Take your hand away and let me see it! I want to help you—let me see it! Sammy, please—don't run around, Sammy—stand still—let me see it! *Will you stand still?* (*She has now made him stand still. She pulls his hand away from his face. Dead silence as she looks. He awaits her verdict suspensefully. At last she speaks with baleful horror.*) . . . Oh, Sammy!

SAM. (*With great misgiving.*) What?

TILDA. Oh, I can't tell you!

SAM. (*His alarm growing.*) What, what?

TILDA. You've lost it . . . the eye is gone.

SAM. Wh-hat?

TILDA. Gone!—nothing there!—I can see clear through to the back of your head!

SAM. (*Offended dignity.*) You certainly cannot see to the back of my head.

TILDA. What's in there to stop me?

SAM. (*Realizing he's been had, he hits at her.*) Why, you—! (*Laughing, she runs away. He chases her, she trips, she falls, he grabs her, she wriggles away, he's after her, they fight like puppies, they laugh a lot. Then he's got her. They're still. They lie together. They catch their breath. They at last both turn quietly and look up at the window. Almost without connecting with one another, their mood has simultaneously changed, reversed itself. They are deeply forlorn and a nameless apprehension has seized them. Slowly* TILDA *rises and, with quiet courage, faces it.*)

TILDA. There's still nobody there . . . except me. (*She goes closer to it and stares at one spot. A reflection of herself. Suddenly she can't stand what she sees. She covers her face with her hands. Quickly he goes to her, tries to take her hands away from her face. She won't let him.*) Don't look at me!

SAM. Tilda—

TILDA. No, don't look at me!

SAM. (*Insistent.*) Yes I will! I'm going to look at you!

TILDA. Don't, please! I'm starting to look ugly again! (*She gets up and runs away.*)

SAM. Tilda— (*He goes after her. He grabs her.*) Tilda, you don't look ugly! Stop looking in that window! In the last minute you haven't changed!—you look exactly as you did before! (*As he forces her to face him, she breaks away.*)

TILDA. Goddamn you, you let me alone! I know when I'm ugly—let me alone! (*Slowly, his hands drop away from her. She turns from him, her face in her hands as if to hide her ugliness not only from him but from herself. Silence. He watches her. At last she takes her hands away from her face. Her expression is entirely serene now.*) I'm sorry . . . You see, you needn't have worried about me. It always passes. (*Then, very tentatively.*) Next time—don't pay any attention.

SAM. Don't be stupid. Of course I will.

TILDA. When I'm behaving that way I don't want you to look at me!

SAM. (*Snapping.*) What shall I do?—act as if you don't exist?

TILDA. Yes!

SAM. (*Angrier—raising his voice.*) Somebody's shrieking to tell me she's not there!

TILDA. That's right!

SAM. No! Get it into your head! When I look at you it's not for your sake, it's for mine! I have to know you're there not because of you but because of me! You're the only sign I've got!

TILDA. (*Very quietly.*) Any minute you'll be shrieking.

SAM. . . . Will I?

TILDA. . . . Yes. (*Silence. His hand goes tentatively to his throat.*)

SAM. . . . I woke up once . . . in the middle of the night . . . and my throat was very sore.

TILDA. (*Worriedly.*) Is it still?

SAM. No, but . . . in the night . . . was I . . . screaming? (*She doesn't answer. He is shaken. To himself.*) Oh, dammit.

TILDA. (*To comfort.*) Only once—and nobody else heard you.

SAM. Like the last time?

TILDA. No, Sammy, not as loud—not as bad.

SAM. Did you make me stop?

TILDA. I think I helped you stop, yes.

SAM. Did I . . . (*This gives him difficulty.*) . . . hurt you?

TILDA. Not a bit, Sammy—you never do—never!

SAM. (*He is relieved. Then:*) Did I say any name?

TILDA. (*Sorry to disappoint him.*) No,

SAM. You sure?

TILDA. Yes, I'm sure.

SAM. Sometimes when I wake up in the morning I feel I've said some name and nobody's been listening. Were you really listening?

TILDA. Honey, there wasn't any name.

SAM. I keep thinking . . . people hear me talking— and making connections—and they won't tell me how I've done it!

TILDA. You think I would do that?

SAM. (*Not sure.*) . . . No . . . Why am I so certain I'm talking to somebody?

TILDA. To whom? Shall we work on it?

SAM. No, it never gets us anywhere.

TILDA. Shall we work on whether it's a man or a woman?

SAM. What good is it? I have no way of knowing!

TILDA. Let's say some names to each other—just any old names—you say one, I say one—without thinking.

SAM. All right . . . Samuel.

TILDA. Why start with your own name?

SAM. Maybe it's not my own name.

TILDA. I'm sure it *is* your name. You want to know what makes me sure of that?—I think you're Jewish.

SAM. (*Amused.*) Jewish?—me?

TILDA. Yes!

SAM. What gave you that idea?

TILDA. Because one day you said you didn't like the Christmas tree.

SAM. (*Wryly.*) Well, that's pretty conclusive, isn't it? Except that I never said I didn't like the Christmas tree —and I'm not Jewish!

TILDA. How can you not be—with a name like Samuel?

SAM. There are lots of Samuels who aren't Jewish. They're Baptists and Presbyterians and Seventh Day Adventists. Besides, you know why I'm certain I'm not a Jew?—I've never been circumcised.

TILDA. There are lots of Jews who haven't been circumcised.

SAM. Name one.

TILDA. Give me a minute.

SAM. Anyway, my name is Samuel.

TILDA. You're satisfied with that name simply because you don't want to remember.

SAM. I do want to remember!

TILDA. Then why not explore the possibilities?—they're endless! You might have been called Bartholomew or Charlemagne or—

SAM. That's enough, Tilda.

TILDA.—or Samson the Magnificent—

SAM. Quit it!

TILDA.—or Carlominius—

SAM. I said stop it!

TILDA.—or Xerxes the Terrible—

SAM. You really want me to leave, don't you?!

TILDA.—or Simon, the Duke of Lusitania—

SAM. No! (*The sharpness of his tone stops her. It alarms her. His voice softens.*) There's nobody with any of those names.

TILDA. It doesn't have to be somebody you *know!*

SAM. (*With a smile.*) Well, that's an answer, isn't it? Somebody I don't know is after me. And the somebody is me. I'm like a dog chasing his own tail.

TILDA. (*As wry as he is.*) It would be funny if it weren't frightening . . . And yet, I'm envious.

SAM. Envious?

TILDA. Yes. You've got people back there. You don't know who they are, you don't know what to call them—but you know they're there. They might be your mother and father—sisters, brothers—anybody! They're almost in the room—just the other side of the window—any minute they'll come through! Maybe some night you'll scream so loud it'll shatter the glass and they'll come rushing in to help you, to comfort you . . . Anyway, they're there . . . you know they are.

SAM. (*Consoling.*) They're there for you too, Tilda.

TILDA. (*Facing a dire fact. With courage.*) No . . .
there's nobody in that window except me.

SAM. But you do remember things!

TILDA. . . . No.

SAM. I can *see* you remembering things! The other day
when I was trying to think of the second president of the
United States you said Adams, without a flicker. Last
night when I said "When to the sessions of sweet silent
thought," you did the rest of the sonnet, the whole thing!

TILDA. Oh, I can remember things like that! You want
me to tell you the tributaries of the Mississippi River? I
can give you every damn one of them! And I can draw
you the whole subway system of New York City—
Brooklyn, Riverdale, Flatbush, Canarsie!—but I don't
know anybody who lives in those places! Oh yes, and
mathematics—I can do you a binomial equation and the
cube root of anything! Except people, Sammy—I don't
know the cube root of people! (*Silence. Then, more con-
trolledly.*) Maybe I never knew any people. Maybe I
never even had a mother. Tilda—immaculately conceived
—*by* no one, out of no one . . .

SAM. (*Gently.*) Would you like some ice cream?

TILDA. No, I don't think so.

SAM. I'll bring you a mountain of it, a whole mountain
of ice cream, with a river of chocolate sauce.

TILDA. You don't have to cheer me up, Sam.

SAM. Shall I paint you a picture?

TILDA. No, thank you.

SAM. I'll paint you one—with every different kind of
smile on it. Did you know that every smile's a different
color?

TILDA. Some of them are gray.

SAM. I'll bring you a newspaper that has no printing
on it. You read whatever news you write!

TILDA. Oh, how terrible!

SAM. I know!—numbers!—you're very good with numbers! I'll write you a set of numbers that are all exactly

right!—just the way they are! You don't have to do anything with them—add them up or subtract them or multiply or divide!—nothing! They're perfectly happy if you let them alone and just . . . (*Tenderly.*) . . . touch them from time to time.

TILDA. . . . So am I, Sammy. (*Slowly he reaches across and touches her. They are very still with each other.*)

SAM. You won't ever leave me, will you, Tilda?

TILDA. (*Very simply.*) No.

SAM. Do you promise that?

TILDA. Yes, I promise.

SAM. You won't go back?

TILDA. Why would I go back?

SAM. If you remembered, you might want to.

TILDA. I won't remember.

SAM. How can you be sure of that?

TILDA. Because . . . I think . . . I've stopped trying.

SAM. Oh no you haven't! Sometimes I see you trying so hard—as if you've only got one minute left to do it in!

TILDA. Never! Me? When?

SAM. . . . When The Person is here.

TILDA. The Person? He doesn't make one bit of difference to me! In fact, when he's here, I try *not* to remember!

SAM. I don't believe that, Tilda.

TILDA. It's true! I don't pay any attention to him!—none at all!

SAM. You do! You watch him, you watch him!

TILDA. I don't! I do not!

SAM. As if you're trying to hear him!

TILDA. That's the rottenest thing—! I could no more listen to The Person—! When he comes, I turn myself against him! And as to listening to him—if you think I'd get caught by one of his tricks—!

SAM. Some day you will!

TILDA. You're wrong, you're wrong!

SAM. I don't think you would do it to hurt me. Or because you *want* to leave me. It'll just happen! The Person will talk—you'll hear him—and it'll all be over!

TILDA. That's impossible!—you want to know why it's impossible?

SAM. Why?

TILDA. Because I know the Person is even worse than you ever imagined he could be.

SAM. Worse?—in what why?

TILDA. (*Very quietly.*) He's our enemy. He turns people against us.

SAM. How do you know that?

TILDA. He's done it to me.

SAM. (*Quiet, but excited.*) How?—when?

TILDA. When I first came here.

SAM. Whom did he turn against you?

TILDA. . . . Tankee . . . and the others.

SAM. Who's Tankee? (*An instant. To overcome her reluctance.*) Who is it?

TILDA. When I first came here, there was nobody here —nobody. I had so much space around me I thought I'd die of it. And I couldn't fill it with anything except . . . me. So one day I made somebody up. The first one was Tankee. For a long while she just stood there in the dark and then she came closer and she was my true friend. She always walked a little bit ahead of me to ward things off. Oh, she was lovely! And then one day, just when I was most comfortable with her, she sickened and died . . . Then I made the twins up. They were a boy and a girl— but you couldn't tell them apart. They were different from Tankee. They weren't as kind-hearted but they were lots of fun—they ran races without ever moving and they pulled practical jokes. Then one day they started to hit me. They pushed me up against a wall and they kicked me and beat me. I kept saying to them: "Why are you doing it? I've always loved you!—why are you hurting me?" And when I couldn't talk any more, they dis-

appeared—they just faded back into the loneliness . . .
And then I realized who was doing those things to me. It
was The Person. He turned all my friends against me.
And you know how he did it? He made *me* do terrible
things to them! I drove them away!

SAM. No—not you, Tilda!

TILDA. Yes—I did it myself! (*Then, quietly.*) When I
realized he was making me do that, I stopped making people up. I just sat there and sat there. And if anybody
started to come into my mind, I made it go dark, I pulled
down the blind! And I thought: there's nobody back
there—and there's nobody here—and there never will be!
—not anywhere!—never! (*She has come to the end of
the unhappy part of her story. Now ever so slowly, her
whole being changes. She is like skies in old Bibles, with
the light coming through clouds.*) And one day I opened
my eyes a little . . . and you were there . . . And
you've never hurt me . . . and never gone away. (*Her
smile returning.*) You don't play baseball very well . . .
but you do everything else as if you had spent your life
learning to please me . . . And now I've thought of a
way to please you.

SAM. (*Gently.*) You always please me, Tildie.

TILDA. No . . . even more . . .

SAM. How?

TILDA. I'm not going to look for my people any more—
I'm going to look for yours . . . As if they were mine.

SAM. (*Quietly.*) No, Tilda.

TILDA. The two of us together—we'll find them.

SAM. I don't want you to, Tilda.

TILDA. You mean you don't want me— (*Searching for
the word.*) —involved in your other life?

SAM. I don't want you involved in some part of my life
that's . . . painful. Whoever those people are they've got
a terrible power . . .

TILDA. What?

SAM. . . . torture.

TILDA. Of course they have. They're people.

SAM. I don't want them to hurt you, Tilda—as they must have hurt me. . . . Or—as I must have hurt them.

TILDA. You didn't—you couldn't!

SAM. Couldn't I? (*Very quietly.*) I might have killed somebody.

TILDA. I don't believe that!

SAM. Yes, I might have, Tilda. Sometimes when I wake up in the night—

TILDA. No!

SAM.—I feel that someone—!

TILDA. No!

SAM. How can I know? I can't remember anybody!

TILDA. Yes, you do!—you remember the boys in the classroom!

SAM. No, not really! I know there are boys there but I don't see any of them! And I don't know what I'm doing there!

TILDA. You're teaching!—you're a teacher!

SAM. What am I teaching? What subject?

TILDA. Why do you chase him away?

SAM. I'm not chasing anybody.

TILDA. Yes you are! You're chasing away the man you're looking for! (*He stops. He looks at her. She has struck a note that echoes in himself.*)

SAM. Am I?

TILDA. Yes. You're so desperate to find him that you're frightening him off . . .

SAM. Perhaps . . . (*Quietly.*) Sometimes I see somebody who seems to belong to him. It's a woman. And I suspect she's his mother. I can't see her face, but she holds her arms in a motherly way. And her voice is soft the way mothers' voices are supposed to be. It's a good moment . . . And any instant she'll turn so the light won't make bad reflections and I'll see her face. But she turns the opposite way . . . and disappears . . . and it doesn't matter where I go, she's not there. And suddenly

I'm moving toward a dark alley and no matter how much I tell myself that I mustn't enter it, I keep moving toward that dark alley—and I know there's a man in there and he's waiting for me. And I know he'll hurt me. He's just waiting there to hurt me. I try to stop myself—to keep myself from going in but I keep going and going and there's nobody to stop me. And I think: any minute I'm going to see his face—and I don't want to see it but I've got to! If only somebody will stop me from going in—can't somebody stop me—? (*He has become tense; his voice, strident. He pauses now, bringing himself under control. Now he speaks softly again.*) When I first came here—in one of the other rooms—when The Person was asking me questions, I made up my mind I'd never tell him about the man in the alley. But then one day—I don't know how it happened—I think he tricked me—I found myself telling him. And do you know what he did, that bastard?—he didn't listen to me at all—he just wrote it down! He had a pad of paper in his hand and he wrote it down! It's on my record now—he's got something against me! (*An instant.*) But from that time on whenever The Person asked me questions I never answered. And pretty soon I couldn't hear him at all! (*An instant, then:*)

TILDA. Sammy . . . last night . . . when you screamed . . . was it the man in the alley?

SAM. I . . . don't know.

TILDA. What does he look like?

SAM. (*Trying to get away from the subject.*) I can't describe him.

TILDA. Is he short, is he tall?

SAM. I don't want to talk about it.

TILDA. I thought if I could help you see him—

SAM. (*An outbreak.*) I don't want to see him! I want to get rid of him!

TILDA. (*Mostly to herself.*) That's funny. If I had somebody, I wouldn't want to get rid of him . . . even if he terrified me.

SAM. (*Trying to make a joke of it.*) You've got me—don't I terrify you?

TILDA. (*Studying the question.*) Yes, you do, sometimes.

SAM. (*Upset by her answer.*) You're joking. (*An instant, then:*)

TILDA. Yes . . . I'm joking. (*They both know she is not joking. It bothers them.*)

SAM. I want to play something.

TILDA. Let's play Enjoying Everything.

SAM. I'm not good at that. You always have more things to enjoy.

TILDA. Well, you just don't look. Yesterday you didn't even see the Christmas tree.

SAM. I saw it! I just didn't make it part of the game! You make all sorts of things part of the game—and you rack up a lot of points that shouldn't qualify—

TILDA. There are always things I enjoy!

SAM. Oh, come on!

TILDA. It's true! I enjoy everything here! I know that's an unfair advantage but I do!

SAM. You expect me to believe—?

TILDA. Name one thing—just name one thing that I listed that I don't enjoy!

SAM. Me!

TILDA. (*Silence. Then, quietly.*) . . . But I do enjoy you, Sammy.

SAM. You can't! I'm a drag!

TILDA. Yes, sometimes you are. But sometimes—when you lose an eye in baseball or when you advise George Washington to lie to his father or when you work it out for Hamlet and Ophelia to live happily ever after in the suburbs of Elsinore—you're not a drag at all.

SAM. I want to play Being Important.

TILDA. (*Groaning.*) Oh, that's a drag.

SAM. (*Pouncing.*) There!—you see?—you see?

TILDA. What kind of Important? Scientific? Political? Historical?

SAM. Oh, historical! With our names on public documents and our voices breaking wind with vast sociological pronouncements—

TILDA. (*She pounces on the word and points her finger at him.*) Sociology! That's it!—Sociology!

SAM. What about it?

TILDA. Sociology!—that was your subject! You taught sociology!

SAM. The hell I did!

TILDA. (*Disappointed.*) You didn't?

SAM. No, I certainly didn't! I don't feel like a sociology teacher! Do I look like a sociology teacher? (*Suddenly she hears someone.*)

TILDA. Listen!

SAM. What?

TILDA. The Person!

SAM. Where?

TILDA. I don't know—but I hear him. (*He looks around quickly. Then, with gentle insistence.*)

SAM. No, Tilda—he's not here.

TILDA. I swear, Sammy—I heard him!

SAM. (*With quiet deliberation.*) But there's nobody here, Tilda. (*Then:*) You mean in the window?

TILDA. No! I do not mean in the window. He's there— really there—the other side of the door. Listening. (*An instant. Her tense voice, her concentrated state of being, convince him. It is now* SAM *who is unnerved.*)

SAM. I hate it when he spies on us! I hate it!

TILDA. Sh . . .

SAM. (*More and more unnerved.*) You see him yet?

TILDA. No.

SAM. Anything? His shadow?

TILDA. (*Wryly.*) He doesn't have any shadow. He pulls it in with him.

SAM. Yes, the bastard!

TILDA. Sh—he'll hear you!

SAM. I don't give a damn!

TILDA. He'll be coming in, Sammy—we better clean the place up.

SAM. Let him see it as it is!

TILDA. I don't want him to see it! What did you do with the bat and the ball?

SAM. Over there. (*She hurries to pick up the imaginary objects.*)

TILDA. Where's the glove, where's the glove?

SAM. I don't know—you were pitching—what did you do with it?

TILDA. (*Distressed.*) I don't know. (*Delighted.*) Here it is. Okay—everything? Is everything cleared up? (SAM's *glance goes to the tree. So does hers.*)

SAM. What'll we do about the tree?

TILDA. Leave it. I hate to take it down.

SAM. What if he sees it?

TILDA. He didn't see it yesterday.

SAM. Yesterday he nearly bumped into it.

TILDA. But he didn't *see* it, did he?

SAM. No.

TILDA. Well, then . . . (*Now simultaneously they hear the foot-steps.*) Oh, God! (*She rushes to her seat.*)

SAM. (*A hushed warning.*) Now, no listening to him, understand!—no listening!

TILDA. Sh!

(SAM *sits in his seat. They are at a distance from one another, both facing straight front. Their faces have gone absolutely expressionless; their bodies not rigid, but totally still. The whole quality of them is: absence . . . Now The Person enters. He is a middle-aged man, pleasant and serious looking. The prepossessing thing about him is the depth of his concern for* SAM *and* TILDA, *a real concern, not in any way ostentatious, in fact, almost reticent. When he looks at them, he really looks. And when he speaks . . . he is not heard. His mouth moves, his*

*expression is that of a man who is really saying
something, not making talk, but what words issue
from his mouth are not audible. They are not audible
to* SAM *and* TILDA—*and they are not audible to us.
So that his mouth is making a dumb show which
looks like quiet, deeply reasoned, deeply felt speech
—all unheard. Now, he enters the room, stops on the
periphery of their living area and smiles. He says
what appears to be "Good morning." Neither* SAM
nor TILDA *stirs.* THE PERSON *says a few more words,
then takes a few steps closer, standing between* SAM
and TILDA. *Again he speaks, pauses for response and
gets none. He nods to one, then to the other, quite
patient with their pointed disregard of him. But now
he does something which makes them both stiffen:
he advances to the very edge of the imaginary Christmas tree area. He is sensitive to the way their bodies
have become alerted; he doesn't know the cause. He
doesn't of course know that the Christmas tree is
there. But he wonders what he has said or done that
has awakened some reaction in them. He directs
questions, now to* TILDA, *now to* SAM, *asking whether
he has said anything they'd like to comment on. Is
there, perhaps, something he has done? But they
continue to disregard him, enjoying the suspense of
whether or not he will have anything to do with
their Christmas tree. Seeing that he is getting no rejoinder at all,* THE PERSON *moves. He walks right
through the Christmas tree! While his back is mo-
mentarily turned to* SAM *and* TILDA, *they gasp at
the sight of him promenading through their tree
and abruptly start to laugh. Not aloud; they stifle
it—just soon enough so that when* THE PERSON
*again turns to them he sees the distant impassive
faces. Now he goes to sit beside* SAM. *He starts to
talk, trying to engage* SAM'S *interest; he doesn't get
it. Meanwhile, as* THE PERSON *talks to* SAM, TILDA

*becomes more relaxed, realizing that she is not at
all under scrutiny. She turns and looks at* SAM. *She
is delighted to see how still he is. Secure that he will
remain that way, she waves to him behind* THE
PERSON'S *back.* SAM *doesn't lose his equanimity.
She makes a face at him. She makes another which
she considers funnier; it is certainly more elaborate.
Now she rises and starts making gestures, assuming
comic positions. Nothing breaks* SAM *up. She is just
about to launch onto her most outlandish monkey-
shine when* THE PERSON *rises. Just in time she resumes her seat—and her vacant expression.* THE
PERSON *hasn't caught her. Now he advances toward*
TILDA. *He says a few words to her, then sits down
in approximately the same relationship to* TILDA *as,
previously, to* SAM. *Again he talks. Again he is
greeted by vacuity.* SAM'S *reaction, as he watches*
THE PERSON *with* TILDA *is quite different than*
TILDA'S *was. There is no fun in it for him—for he is
not nearly so certain of* TILDA'S *independence of*
THE PERSON *as he is of his own. He watches them
closely, even somewhat tensely, his muscles tighter
than* TILDA'S. *At last* THE PERSON *gives up for the
moment and rises. As he does,* SAM'S *relief is visible.*
THE PERSON *says a few parting words to both of
them, and, departing, walks right through the Christmas tree again.* SAM *and* TILDA *can hardly contain
their laughter. The instant they feel secure* THE
PERSON *is out of earshot, they burst into gales.*)

SAM. Did you see him?—did you see him?—he walked
right through the tree!

TILDA. Twice!—he walked through it twice!

SAM. Straight through!—gangway!—straight through!

TILDA. I thought I would die! How could he miss it?
—it's ten feet tall!

SAM. Right   through   it!—limbs—branches—right
through it!

TILDA. I told you he wouldn't see it!

SAM. But why didn't he? What's the matter with him? —is he stupid?

TILDA. (*Suddenly serious.*) . . . Maybe he's blind.

SAM. (*Puzzling it.*) . . . I don't think so. He's no different than the others. They see things but they don't know they're there. A big tree like that—how can they miss it?

TILDA. They don't see the tree for the woods.

SAM. That doesn't make sense.

TILDA. Of course it doesn't. That's why it's true.

SAM. (*Quickly.*) When he was sitting beside you, did you hear what he was saying?

TILDA. No, of course not.

SAM. Not a word?

TILDA. Not a word. (*With a start.*) Why?—did you?

SAM. No, I couldn't hear a whisper! (*Smiling but annoyed.*) But I swear, the next time you make faces at me, I'm going to stand up—while he's sitting there—and make faces right back at you!

TILDA. Don't you dare!

SAM. Well, don't do it any more!

TILDA. Why? I'm not afraid—you won't listen to him!—I've got confidence in you.

SAM. It's yourself you don't have confidence in.

TILDA. (*Playfully.*) Yes I do, yes I do!

SAM. (*Sobering.*) You know what occurred to me?— maybe the joke's on us. Maybe we *are* listening . . . and the reason we don't hear him is: he's not talking. (*They look at each other for an alarmed moment. Then she laughs uneasily.*)

TILDA. That's a ridiculous idea—he *is* talking.

SAM. How do you know?

TILDA. His lips were moving.

SAM. (*Sharply.*) How do you know that?—did you look at him?

TILDA. (*Defensively.*) Not a bit. I didn't even turn in his direction.

SAM. Are you sure?

TILDA. Of course I'm sure. You don't think I'd say I turned in his direction if I didn't!

SAM. Then how do you know if his lips were moving?

TILDA. I could see it—out of the corner of my eye. I had a sense of it. I could feel it!

SAM. (*Something disquieting hits him.*) If he thinks he's going to get us back there by his sneaky little visits every day—! (*Without warning, he loses control. He rushes back in the direction that* THE PERSON *has gone and shouts.*) You're not getting us back there! You hear me? Hey— Hey—you— Person!—you're not going to throw us out of here! We're here to stay! You hear me?

TILDA. Sh—gently—gently!

SAM. You hear me?

TILDA. If you don't want to hear them, don't ask them to hear you!

SAM. (*It gets through to him.*) Why does he always come so early in the morning? Why do we have to start the day off with him?

TILDA. He wants to see how we've come through the night.

SAM. To see if we've killed each other.

TILDA. Do you suppose he watches us *during* the night?

SAM. Yes. I think so.

TILDA. We'll never be private, will we?

SAM. . . . No.

TILDA. Do you mind very much?

SAM. Yes.

TILDA. Why?

SAM. You know why.

TILDA. (*Quietly.*) For sex, you mean?

SAM. Yes.

TILDA. (*An animated inspiration, to avoid the seriousness.*) I know what we can do! We can confuse the hell out of that bastard! Some night—in the dark—we'll make him think we *are* having sex! We'll groan and moan and make a hundred ridiculous noises! We'll get him so mixed up!—we'll have the son of a bitch in a straitjacket by morning!

SAM. (*Soberly.*) Very funny, but I wasn't talking about pretend sex. I mean real.

TILDA. (*Also sobering.*) I know that's what you mean.

SAM. Well?

TILDA. Does it really mean that much to you, Sammy?

SAM. Doesn't it to you?

TILDA. No, because I've already had pretend sex with you.

SAM. . . . and it was terrible.

TILDA. No, it was wonderful. It was so wonderful that . . .

SAM. . . . nothing can be as good. (*Silence. She cannot meet this confrontation.*) Answer me.

TILDA. (*Unhappily.*) Yes, that's right. (*With a mirthless smile.*) I'm sure that's a great deal worse than talking to myself. (*Seeing how distressed she is, he tenderly takes her in his arms. He kisses her gently, very gently, on the mouth.*)

SAM. Your toothpaste smells like cloves.

TILDA. Then it's not mine. Mine smells like peppermint.

SAM. Then you've been brushing somebody else's teeth. (*He kisses her again. She starts to quake.*)

TILDA. Oh, maybe now!—maybe now! Let me go— maybe now! (*She breaks away from him and rushes to the imaginary window.*)

SAM. Now what?

TILDA. Now!—when I'm feeling something! (*Urgently she exhorts her reflection in the imaginary window.*) You, there!—in the window!—he just kissed you!—don't you look any prettier now? You can't let a kiss go by for nothing! It's got to make a difference!—it's got to make you beautiful! Don't you feel any prettier? (*What she sees is forlornly the same. She is about to cry.*) No . . . you're just as you were.

SAM. (*Gently.*) Come back, Tilda.

TILDA. No.

SAM. Come, honey. (*Reluctantly she returns. Quietly she goes into his arms. In silence he comforts her. When she comes out of his arms, she is completely recovered.*)

TILDA. Thank you, Sammy. (*Startled. With sudden remembrance.*) The visitors! Do you remember how the visitors were always trying to get their arms around us?

SAM. (*Alarmed: she's remembering something; he isn't.*) Visitors?—no! Back there?

TILDA. No—here—in the other rooms!

SAM. (*Quickly.*) What do you remember about them?

TILDA. (*Disturbed.*) I don't know!— I couldn't recognize any of them! But oh, I felt so sorry for them. They aways looked so tired! As if the trip had been so long and they'd had to get up before daylight to catch the train—and it was a local and it stopped everywhere—and there was no food in the diner. And when they'd see me they wouldn't know what to say and they'd just sit there looking so sad and dejected I would ache for them. And all the time I knew that what they wanted most in the world was to get out of here and get back on that slow, bad train and go straight home again. And I had the feeling that every one of them had a terrible, terrible secret and they were afraid I'd find out. Oh, I couldn't bear those poor visitors! (*It's too upsetting.*) Let's do the tree!

SAM. Oh, hell yes—let's do the tree!

TILDA. (*Dithering.*) May I go to the top, may I go to the top?

SAM. Did you do the angel?

TILDA. I don't know whether I did her, but she's done! (*She climbs the tree, singing "Take Me Out to the Ball Game." She affixes the angel to the top of the tree.*) Is she on all right?

SAM. Yes, if she's supposed to be drunk. Here's another strand of lights—grab hold.

TILDA. No—wait!

SAM. Wait for what? Tilda? (*Still no answer. He now turns and notices her manner. She is looking into the tree. She seems hypnotized by what she sees. And terrified.*) Tilda . . . ? (*Silence.*) Tilda—what's the matter?

TILDA. (*Almost mute.*) . . . Look.

SAM. Look at what?

TILDA. Look . . . look! (*Then a stifled scream.*) Oh, look!

SAM. Tilda!—what is it!—Tilda!

TILDA. Help me—help me!

SAM. Tilda, come down!

TILDA. Help me! I'm going to fall!—help me! (*He rushes to her and helps her down. She is shaking with fright.*)

SAM. Tilda, what is it? Tilda! Tilda, honey—please—what is it? Talk! Tilda!

TILDA. There . . . was . . . something . . . in the tree.

SAM. What? In the tree? What?

TILDA. Something. Someone.

SAM. Who?

TILDA. A face. I saw somebody's face. Up there—in the branches—I saw it.

SAM. (*He looks quickly at the tree, then to* TILDA.) There's nobody there, Tilda.

TILDA. I saw her.

SAM. The angel, you mean?

TILDA. No. It hadn't anything to do with the angel. It was a face. (*Then shaking dread.*) It was a little girl's face.

SAM. A little girl?

TILDA. Yes, in the tree! I was decorating my side and she was doing hers! And she smiled at me.

SAM. (*Quietly. The Sane reasoning with the Insane.*) Don't be upset, Tilda. There's nobody there.

TILDA. (*In a burst of rage.*) Don't you think I know that? Do you have to talk to me the way they do? Nicely?

Sensibly? Humoring me? (*Lashing at him—imitating the reasonableness of his voice.*) "Don't be upset, Tilda. There's nobody there." What do I get upset by?—whether she's there or whether I see her?! Well, I'll tell you the answer to that! I don't see her because she's there!—she's there because I see her!—and from now on she'll always be in that tree! (*Silence. He waits a long while before speaking. Then, very softly:*)

SAM. Who is she, Tilda?

TILDA. (*Suddenly quiet again. Miserably.*) I don't know.

SAM. (*Not pressing her.*) You said she was a little girl. How old?

TILDA. I don't know. Four. Maybe five.

SAM. What did she look like?

TILDA. (*Her misery deepening.*) You know what she looked like. (*She starts to cry.*) . . . Except she was . . . happy.

SAM. (*Almost a whisper.*) I'm sure you were happy, Tilda, when you were her age. You know how I know that? Because you still are.

TILDA. Well, one thing I know, I'll never go up that ladder again!

SAM. Yes you will.

TILDA. Not me. I don't want to see her any more!

SAM. You won't see her. (*Pointing to the tree.*) Go on.

TILDA. No! I don't want to remember anybody!

SAM. If you remember, you remember—there's no avoiding it!

TILDA. (*A sudden thought.*) Wait! Maybe I wasn't remembering. Maybe I made her up.

SAM. (*Vaguely he feels the need to warn her.*) Tilda . . .

TILDA. Maybe I did! The way I made up Tankee and The Twins! Maybe I made her up! (*Then with a shudder.*) And maybe she'll get sick the way Tankee did . . . or maybe she'll hit me . . .

SAM. Would you rather think you made her up?—or you remembered her?

TILDA. Remembering hurts!

SAM. So did Tankee! Choose one or the other.

TILDA. Are those the only choices? (*They look at one another. Neither has an answer.*)

SAM. You've absolutely decided—you're not going up the tree?

TILDA. No—never!

SAM. (*Going into action, starting toward the tree.*) Well, then, let's take the tree down.

TILDA. (*Alarmed.*) No!— It's beautiful!

SAM. (*Hotly.*) Well, it's not going to stay beautiful if we ascribe terrible things to it!

TILDA. I'm going up the Goddamn ladder!

SAM. (*An instant. Hiding his delight and his surprise.*) . . . You are? (*She is at the foot of the ladder, unmistakably apprehensive.*)

TILDA. Don't go away.

SAM. I won't, honey. (*Slowly, slowly, her dread plain, she ascends one level. She stops an instant, looks down at him, reveals her temptation to descend again, conquers it and continues slowly, valiantly to the top. She is looking for the face of the child. After a long moment.*) . . . Well?

TILDA. She . . . she's not there.

SAM. (*Relieved for her.*) There—you see? Nothing to be frightened of.

TILDA. Yes . . . nothing. (*She holds the stillness.*) I wish she were there. She was happy. And she was . . . somebody. (*They exchange a glance.*) Hand me another strand of lights. (*He hands her a strand and she busies herself, stringing it up. He has suddenly gone absent. Caught by something else. Something he hears, something he sees. He makes a sharp, sudden gesture as if he's trying to drive something away. It's as if it were an insect first, then something larger and more terrifying. TILDA is turned away and doesn't notice. Abruptly* SAM'S *seizure passes. He looks at* TILDA *to see if she has caught him in it. She hasn't. Silent and subdued, he stands there, motionless. Again his sudden gesture—almost spastic now, convulsing his whole body—to drive the terrorist away. Again, silence. Stiff, taut, an unearthly look in his eyes, he starts to whistle. A simple melody, but eerie, desolate.* TILDA *hears it and looks at him.*) What's that you're whistling? (SAM *doesn't answer.*) Sammy, what is it?

SAM. It's . . . nothing. (*He starts to whistle again. She listens, then:*)

TILDA. It's weird—what is it?

SAM. (*Irritably.*) It's nothing—it's a song! (*He tries to capture it again—one melody, another. He's lost it.*) Damn you, you made me lose it!

TILDA. What was it?

SAM. (*His irritation growing.*) Nothing—a phrase of music!—why did you have to interfere?

TILDA. Music!—you were a music teacher!

SAM. (*Losing control.*) Why don't you shut up?!

TILDA. Sammy—

SAM. Shut up, shut up!—why don't you shut up!

TILDA. I'm just trying to help you!

SAM. Why do you have to help me? Help me do what? —get out of here? You trying to get rid of me? Why do you have to help me?

TILDA. (*Meeting his rage with her own.*) Because I can't bear to see how unhappy you are! You're killing yourself trying to remember—and I can't bear it!

SAM. (*Trying to control himself.*) Look, you've got something wrong! You act as if we're here because we *have* to be here! Maybe you are—maybe you're here without a choice—you're here by default! But I'm not! I can get out whenever I want to! (*The boast is desperate because he knows it's untrue.*) *I've got a choice!*

TILDA. Choice? Who gives you a choice? What choice?

SAM. Whether to stay here—or go back there and kill somebody!

TILDA. You wouldn't kill anybody!

SAM. Maybe I've already done it! (*The sudden and terrible possibility.*) Oh, God, maybe I have!

TILDA. No, Sammy! (*His seizure is total. He starts to kill. It is a small but awful gesture: he rips some imaginary object with clenched hands; again and again he rips it; his face contorted with a self-afflicting fury. He makes strangled cries. She tries to stop him, she can't.*) Sammy! Sammy—no! Don't—don't—Sammy—please! (*At last she brings him under control. For an instant he does not recognize her. Then, abruptly, he does. The seizure not yet entirely over, he pulls her into his arms.*) Oh, Tilda! . . . Tilda, don't leave me!

TILDA. No—no, I won't—no!

SAM. Don't ever leave me!

TILDA. No—I promise—no!

SAM. If you ever leave me— (*Still partly in the seizure, he grabs her by the throat. He might strangle her if it weren't for what she does: nothing! She remains absolutely still, her hands at her sides, giving herself to his mercy. Slowly, his tension subsides. He releases her. He moves away. Stillness. The melody comes back to him. He hums it almost inaudibly. Then:*) . . . You just stood there.

TILDA. Yes.

SAM. You didn't try to protect yourself . . . you didn't try to pull my hands away . . .

TILDA. No.

SAM. My God, you didn't even say "Stop it!" (*To himself.*) Christ!

TILDA. You're contemptuous of that, aren't you?

SAM. What?

TILDA. You've got contempt for me because I was so meek. That's right isn't it?—contempt?

SAM. . . . No.

TILDA. Yes you have! Because you think I'm a submissive little whipped dog who's so devoted to you that I'd let you kill me! If I thought you were going to try,

no matter how much I love you, I'd fight back with my
hands, with my feet, I'd claw you bloody, I'd claw you to
death! But I wasn't afraid you were going to kill me!—
not a Goddamn bit! You may be afraid of the killer in
you—but I'm not! You know why?—because the killer
isn't there! You're not a killer, Sammy! You're a kind,
loving, decent man! Get that into your head! You're not
a killer! (*She doesn't realize he has again spun out of
orbit. His eyes have gone wild.*)

SAM. No—I won't kill him if he doesn't kill me!

TILDA. What?

SAM. He's been after me! Whenever I turn around he's
there! He chases me!

TILDA. Sammy—!

SAM. Tell him to let me alone! (*Whirling.*) Let me
alone!

TILDA. Sammy—Sammy—

SAM. Let me alone—tell me who you are—

TILDA. There's nobody, Sammy—there's nobody there!

SAM. I don't know anybody's name! Tell me somebody's name!

TILDA. Sammy—please— (*As she tries to bring him to
himself, as she tries to help him manage his terror and
his rage, he deals with it alone—and violently. He tries to
find the identity of his assailant; yet, to flee him. He is
now terrified; now himself the terror. He does not flail
aimlessly at the air, but at a specific enemy; what is to
him a tangible, albeit elusive, horror.*)

SAM. Who are you? Tell me who you are! Show me
your face—let me see who you are! No, don't hurt me!—
let me alone! What've you got to do with me? Why do
you want to hurt me?—why? Tell me who you are!
Please! Please! No—please—no! I'll kill you, I'll kill
you! No—who are you? Who are you, who are you, who
are you? You bastard, come through the window! Somebody, help me! Help me! Hey, you—*Person!* (*He has
been raging, battling, weeping. She has been trying to
bring him to reason. Now she is locked to him, holding*

*him with all her strength. Just as he breaks away and
falls to the floor,* THE PERSON *rushes in. As* THE PER-
SON *kneels to help* SAM, TILDA *stands over them, sobbing.*
SAM *is now quite still.* THE PERSON *is ministering to him,
speaking to him. The place is still save for the diminishing
sound of* TILDA'S *weeping. Now, gently,* THE PERSON
helps SAM *to arise. Supporting* SAM'S *weakened body,* THE
PERSON *guides the young man to the same seat he
formerly occupied when* THE PERSON *came to speak to
him.* THE PERSON *too sits down.* SAM *is altogether still,
nothing as yet registering in his eyes. Now* THE PERSON
*starts to talk to him. We still do not hear what he says,
we merely see his lips move. But his manner is all comfort
and conciliation. Moment by moment, awareness comes to*
SAM'S *eyes, then the glimmer of reality; finally, the
struggle of whether or not to listen to* THE PERSON. *At
last, his need great,* SAM *turns his entire body and starts
to listen. We hear a sharp intake of breath from* TILDA.)

TILDA. (*In a low, horrified murmur.*) No . . . no . . .
no . . .

(*Slowly, slowly* SAM *has been turning his body—all his
attention—away from* TILDA *and toward* THE PER-
SON. TILDA *is transfixed with dismay. The tiniest of
sounds emanates from her . . . a sob, a nameless
murmur.*)

END OF ACT ONE

ACT TWO

The following morning. SAM *and* TILDA *are again asleep. Again she is the first to awaken. She discovers her whereabouts and as she contemplates* SAM, *her eyes are grave. But she routs sobriety and forces herself to be cheerful.*

TILDA. Good morning! Good morning, Sammy! (*With forced gaiety, talking to herself.*) Good morning, Tilda— how are you this morning? Now, let's see—how am I? I think if I don't know how I am and don't think of how the rest of the world is, I'm fine and they're fine—and let's leave it that way! (*She looks at him—will he wake up? She gives up singing and talks.*) Sammy, wake up. I told you not to take that capsule—I told you it was a sleeping pill. They don't give you anything to keep awake around here or make you more aware of anything—or livelier! Just deader! It's a cheat! They cheat us out of half our awareness. I wonder what they do with the half they take away? Put it in a refrigerator maybe. Keep it cool . . . and calm. And put a label on it: Tilda—half her awareness. (*She turns to them angrily.*) You dirty bastards, you're stealing half of my life! (*She returns to* SAM.) I won't let them do that to you, Sammy. Not the way those others are in the other rooms—just sitting there in a chair doing nothing, *staring!* We won't let that happen, will we? Wake up, Sammy—wake up! (*He stirs fitfully; makes no sound; doesn't want to be awakened.*) Sammy, did you listen to The Person yesterday?—did you? You looked like you were listening, but I can't believe you were! You weren't, were you? (*She sits beside him, cradles him in her arms.*) If you tell me you were, I'll understand, Sammy—I will—really I'll understand.

43

But please tell me you weren't. (*When he doesn't answer, she gently pushes his head from side to side, making it say no.*) There—I knew you weren't listening to him. Sammy, wake up . . . Sammy.

SAM. (*Stirring a little.*) Honey, let me alone . . . let me sleep.

TILDA. Wake up. Beat the capsule—wake up!

SAM. Please . . . let me sleep.

TILDA. (*Rocking him.*) Okay—sleep. But I don't want you to think a capsule did it to you. Somebody who loves you put you to sleep. Somebody took you in her arms and sang you a lullaby and put you to sleep. (*She forlornly sings Take Me Out to the Ball Game.*) And while you're sleeping I'm going to do the Christmas tree. And when you wake up what a surprise you'll have! It'll shine and glow and the ornaments will twinkle and everywhere you look there'll be happiness! You won't be able to find a dark spot or a corner anywhere! Your eyes will dazzle with happiness! And it won't be any reflections in a window either!—it'll be real! (*Gently she disengages herself from him and lets him sleep. She looks at the window a moment, then goes to the tree. The closer she gets, the more tentative are her footsteps. As she reaches it, she looks in among the branches . . . Will she see the child? Whispering.*) Hello . . . Is someone there? . . . Little girl—? . . . Are you there? . . . Please come back. I promise I won't scream this time. And I won't be afraid. I'll just ask you a few questions. Not hard ones—easy ones, like what's your name? It'll be a game, like Twenty Questions and I'll say, "Are you alive or dead? Do you live in a house I could find my way in? Was I ever a happy as you are?" (*Then apprehensively.*) Are you me? (*Trying to lighten her mood.*) Easy questions like that . . . Then I'll say, "Tell me whatever you want to tell me—tell me about your mother. Do you call her Mother or Ma or Mama. I think if I had a mother I'd call her Mama. Mama—yes—I like that the best. (*Long moment.*) Are you there? Will you ever come back? Please come back

. . . please. I won't tell anybody you're here—I promise I won't. Not even Sammy. Will you ever come back? Oh, please! (*Suddenly, to shake her unhappy mood.*) Gosh, it's warm in here! I have too many clothes on! (*She is taking all her clothes off—not actually, but in her imagination—unaware that* SAM *has awakened and has been quietly watching her. Now she becomes suddenly aware of him, is startled and embarrassed.*) Oh!—a peeping Tom!

SAM. What were you doing?—stripping?

TILDA. Don't be vulgar.

SAM. Shoes stockings, everything. Were you having fun?

TILDA. . . . Yes.

SAM. I'm sorry I spoiled it. I'll go back to sleep and you can strip as much as you like.

TILDA. (*Almost shy at having to say it.*) You don't have to . . . I've already done it.

SAM. Done what?

TILDA. Stripped.

SAM. You have?

TILDA. (*Too diffident to face him.*) . . . Yes . . . I've taken everything off. There isn't anything about me you haven't already seen. Everything I am. Glove by glove, I've thrown away every one of my secrets. There isn't anything I haven't told you. I've taken off every false eyelash. What I've told you isn't much—but it's everything I know about myself. I wish I knew more—just so you would know it too. I love you, Sammy. . . . and I'm totally naked. . . . Touch me. (*She does not look at him. Slowly he rises, moves behind the box she sits on and stands behind her. Gently, ever so gently, he places his two hands on her cheeks. Quickly she raises her hands and clutches his hands more tightly to herself. She quivers in a rhapsody that is as full as love-making. It is almost unbearable to her.*)

SAM. I love you, Tilda.

TILDA. I know you do—but I didn't think you knew it.

SAM. I've known it for a long time.

TILDA. You've never said it . . . and I almost wish you hadn't said it now.

SAM. Do you?—I'll take it back. I don't love you at all.

TILDA. No, I mean it.

SAM. Why?

TILDA. I read a poem once—it said that love is either burning or dying and when a man says "I love you" the flame has gone out and those three words are the smoke of it.

SAM. I'll never say it to you again.

TILDA. Did I make you say that? Isn't it sad?—we want love to be so alive that we kill it. (*She turns a little away from him.*) I had a terrible dream last night.

SAM. What was it?

TILDA. (*Carefully.*) The Person came in and we both sat down and he didn't even try to talk to me. He went straight to you. He talked and he talked—but you didn't listen. And then slowly, ever so slowly, your head turned to him and you did listen. And you heard every word he said. And then . . . *you* began to talk to *him* . . .

SAM. It was only a dream.

TILDA. (*Turning back to him, her eyes very level.*) Are you sure?

SAM. I didn't talk to him. Not one word.

TILDA. But you did listen. (*She waits for an answer. None comes.*) You did, didn't you?

SAM. I didn't intentionally listen, Tilda.

TILDA. Did you hear anything?

SAM. No.

TILDA. Oh, I'm glad!

SAM. Well . . . not much anyway.

TILDA. You mean you did hear something?

SAM. I'm not sure . . . If I did it was only . . . I think I heard him say one word.

TILDA. What word?

SAM. I . . . can't remember it.

TILDA. One word and you can't . . . ?

SAM. No.

TILDA. (*Quickly.*) Then don't try! Sammy, stop frowning. Whatever word he told you, it's not worth hurting yourself to recall it! Now, don't try—please don't try!

SAM. (*He smiles at the spate of her words, at her anxiety.*) All right.

TILDA. Oh, I'm so angry at him—! You see what he does? Now, Sammy, the next time he comes, don't you listen to him!

SAM. I told you I didn't listen on purpose. And if I *hear* him again, that won't be on purpose either!

TILDA. You've got to *not listen* on purpose!

SAM. (*Patting his head and rubbing his stomach.*) That's like patting my mind and rubbing my will power at the same time.

TILDA. (*A pompous pep talk.*) You can do it! You're one of our foremost boys—and I have the utmost confidence in you!

SAM. Thank you, sir, I'll try not to let you down. (*Pleasantly.*) I had a dream too.

TILDA. (*Alerted.*) What kind?

SAM. (*With quick reassurance.*) Oh, it was a nice dream. I was on the ground. I was buried.

TILDA. (*Doubtfully.*) That sounds like a *very* nice dream.

SAM. It was! I was a radish.

TILDA. It's getting nicer and nicer.

SAM. I was a happy radish. Have you ever been a radish?

TILDA. Not a happy one, no.

SAM. An unhappy one?

TILDA. What would make a radish unhappy?

SAM. It he didn't fulfill himself—his hope, his aspiration, his dream.

TILDA. If he didn't fulfill his dream, he'd have to sublimate, wouldn't he?

SAM. Yes. Or fulfill the dream of somebody else. Say, a carrot or a turnip.

TILDA. I notice you choose only things that are buried

in the ground. Suppose he wanted to fulfill the dream of something not so earthbound—something skyborne—a bird!

SAM. That's what makes an unhappy radish.

TILDA. And he dies unhappy.

SAM. Everybody dies unhappy.

TILDA. I don't think of dying much, do you?

SAM. Yes, I die a lot.

TILDA. I used to, I think. I couldn't imagine it so I had to think of Death as a human being. Somebody mysterious—he'd have to come out of the darkness. I imagined him once as a dope pusher in a hallway. And then he was a motor-cycle cop—at night—all dressed in black. One moment he wasn't there and the next moment he was a roar!—-vrroom!—out of the blackness!—"Halt!" . . . Then he was a rapist, with a long silk stocking in his hand—hiding in the entrance to the subway. "Come here, kid, come here." . . . But the most terrifying . . . One day I realized I hadn't any father—at least I couldn't remember him . . . and from that day on, death was my father. (*Stillness.*) But I hardly ever think of it any more. You know why?—it doesn't exist!

SAM. No death?

TILDA. No death! It's another delusion we've been scaring ourselves with!

SAM. (*Only half joking.*) No life either then, huh?

TILDA. (*Shocked.*) Well—no!—hey, that's going too far!

SAM. Maybe we're not supposed to know whether it's true or not. Maybe that's another illusion we've been nursing—that one day we'll find the answer to something. Maybe we're not people . . . only shadows . . . reflections in the window.

TILDA. Reflections don't speak.

SAM. Maybe we only *think* we hear each other speak. Maybe even that's an illusion. No voices—only echoes.

TILDA. Yes. (*Her voice echoing.*) Hello!

SAM. Hello!

TILDA. Hello-oh-oh-oh! (*The ohs, clear and cheery at first, dwindle into the far distance, mournful and desolate.* TILDA *is frightened and forlorn.*) Did my voice make you sad?

SAM. No.

TILDA. It made me sad.

SAM. (*To cheer her.*) Shall we do some more on the tree?

TILDA. (*Disappointed.*) You didn't notice?

SAM. What?

TILDA. How much I've done.

SAM. While I was asleep?

TILDA. Yes.

SAM. You didn't finish it, did you?

TILDA. No . . . Can't you tell how much I did?

SAM. You're disappointed because I couldn't tell.

TILDA. (*Of course she is—but—quickly.*) No, no!

SAM. Yes, you are. Now, come on, you can't really expect me to know how much you did if you did it without me.

TILDA. No—of course not! (*Then, edgily.*) But I did expect you to like it.

SAM. I do! I think it's beautiful! Everything! The silver bells!—especially the arrangement of the sparklers!

TILDA. (*Interrupting flatly.*) There aren't any sparklers. (*He studies her without any immediate rejoinder. Then, gently:*)

SAM. What's the matter, Tilda?

TILDA. I'd rather you said you don't like it than pretend you do.

SAM. I do like it! It's just that I was out of it—and I'm trying to get back in—and you won't let me!

TILDA. You didn't used to *pretend* your way in!—you were there!

SAM. I still am! Nothing's changed!

TILDA. Don't tell me!

SAM. (*As angry as she is now.*) Nothing's changed!— nothing! I didn't listen to The Person! At least I didn't try! And the one thing he said to me I've forgotten! What did I do wrong? What should I have done? If I didn't do it right let's pretend I did! (*She starts to respond but doesn't find an answer. She is confused and visibly shaken. At last she pulls herself together.*)

TILDA. I'm sorry, Sam. (*There is an instant's silence. Then he says one word:*)

SAM. Jess!

TILDA. What?

SAM. That was what he said: Jess.

TILDA. What's a jess?

SAM. It's a name. (*A chill strikes her.*)

TILDA. . . . Of course.

SAM. I think it's . . . a . . . woman's name.

TILDA. (*Quickly.*) Not necessarily. Jess can be a boy's name too. I can remember a boy at school—he used to cheat in arithmetic tests—and he'd put crumpled graham crackers down my blouse—his name was Jessie Stonnicker.

SAM. Did you really know a boy named Jessie Stonnicker?

TILDA. (*Embarrassed.*) No . . . I just made it up. (*Quickly.*) But Jess *can* be a boy's name!

SAM. Yes it can.

TILDA. Then why do you—just like that—say it's a woman's name? Holy mackerel, it might be the name of a dog or a cat.

SAM. (*Sharply.*) All right! Let's say a dog or a cat.

TILDA. Did it make you feel better to think it was a woman?

SAM. No.

TILDA. Because if it makes you feel better we'll imagine it a woman.

SAM. No, the only thing that would make me feel better would be to *know.*

TILDA. Well, The Person won't tell you—don't you rely on *him!* There's nothing they know back there that could possibly make you feel better!

SAM. (*Uncertainly.*) I . . . suppose you're right.

TILDA. As a matter of fact—for all you know—he might have made the name up.

SAM. Made it up?

TILDA. Yes. Simply pulled the name out of a hat! "Oh, by the way, Jesse was a asking for you." Jesse Who?—Jesse What? If anybody says something like that to you, you want to know more, you ask more questions! And the minute you ask the first question, he's got you hooked!

SAM. He hasn't got me hooked.

TILDA. Don't be so cocky about it. Just watch out.

SAM. (*Stubbornly.*) He hasn't got me hooked.

TILDA. He's already done something to you! Before you know it, you'll be trapped!

SAM. Stop it!—I won't be trapped!

TILDA. (*Gearing back a little, she forces herself to be more rational.*) Now listen to me, Sammy. Don't you see what the technique is? He gives you one word. It's a come-on. It teases your mind, it upsets your guts. It makes you want more. Tell me more, tell me more!—who is it I'm trying to remember? What is she to me? Is she connected to somebody else that I know? Do they all live together in my mind? What are they saying? Is it something I'm supposed to understand? What do they mean—what do they mean?! . . . And something tells you that what they mean is pain and you don't listen any more. But pretty soon the pain of not knowing is worse—and you swap one pain for another—and you find out who they are! But what you've found is that you've made a bad deal—you've been cheated! What you've discovered about them isn't anything you want to know! It only has to do with breakfast dishes and locking the doors at night and how many checks you can write before you're over-drawn at the bank! And you grab hold of somebody and you say, "You bastard, that's not what I want to know! I want to know why we should love one another when we both know that love is the worst agony that ever was!

And don't you tell me how Goddamn beautiful life is until
you tell me why we die!—and is dying the whole purpose?! And I want to know about God—if He's there,
why can't we find Him?—and if He's not there, why
can't we get rid of Him? And if you say everything has
a purpose in the world—*what is the use of pain?"* (*Having
started with the intent to remain rational, she has now
unleashed her pain and rage. She becomes aware of it and
pulls herself back under control.*) Questions like that . . .
none of which get answered. Although The Person has
implied that you will get an answer. That was the implica-
tion of the one word. And if you pay attention to it this
time, next time he'll drop another word in your ear . . . to
tantalize you. Then another and another. And pretty soon,
he won't be the only one who's talking . . .

SAM. (*Quietly.*) If you think I'll ever talk to him . . .

TILDA. Yes, you will. You'll start by asking him a question: who is Jesse? And then: who are all the others? And
he'll tell you. Oh, it'll seem as though you're telling *yourself* who you are. But that's a lie—he'll do the telling!
And in the end you'll be the person he tells you you are!
And you'll be right back there, where you started from
. . . playing a part that somebody assigned you . . .
making other people's motions because you're too
frightened to be still.

SAM. You cry before either of us is hurt.

TILDA. (*Angry.*) I am not crying!

SAM. Yes you are! You act as if you could stand up to
The Person very well—but I couldn't! Why? Are you so
unsure about what we've got between us that you're afraid
of my asking him one question: who is Jesse?

TILDA. Yes I am! (*It is self-damning and she realizes
it; but she doesn't flinch from it.*)

SAM. (*Mordantly.*) Then maybe that's the reason
you're the one has to say "I love you" a thousand times
a day and I've only said it once. Because you've got to
hear the sound of the words before you believe them.
You don't say them for me to hear. You say them to

convince your *Self*. Well, I don't have to convince myself. Nothing can shake my conviction that I love you—not a Goddamn thing. Not even The Person. Certainly not the answer to one small question.

TILDA. . . . Small?

SAM. Small, yes.

TILDA. It might be no bigger than a needle—but it can let the blood out.

SAM. Then the blood is thin. (*A long instant. They both realize her next question is inevitable. She does not want to ask it; he does not want to hear it.*)

TILDA. Then you're going to listen to him?

SAM. . . . I think so, yes. (*She suddenly doubles over. He hurries to her in alarm.*) Tilda!

TILDA. (*Straightening up—moving away from him.*) Don't touch me! I just found out something about you.

SAM. What?

TILDA. Yesterday, when you had your hands around my neck—I think you really could have killed me. (*He takes an instant to recover from this. Then:*)

SAM. I didn't though, did I?

TILDA. No, you didn't. But I wonder how much more provocation it would take to make you . . . (*She cannot say it.*)

SAM. Violent.

TILDA. Yes.

SAM. (*With quietest severity.*) Don't be so superior to violence, Tilda.

TILDA. What does that mean?

SAM. You act so holier-than-thou . . . as if you've got no violence in you.

TILDA. . . . Yes, I have . . . But none for you, Sam.

SAM. You're trying to make me feel more and more ashamed of myself, aren't you?

TILDA. I couldn't hurt you, Sammy . . . Except perhaps pretend.

SAM. But pretend is everything to you . . . isn't it?

(*It is of course unanswerable. He goes on.*) And if you hurt me—in pretense—it could be worse than real . . . Because there aren't any limits to "pretend"—are there?

TILDA. (*Very simply.*) Then I won't hurt you in any way, Sammy—not real and not pretend.

SAM. (*In an outburst.*) Stop it! Stop making me feel so Goddamn ashamed of myself! I won't talk to him—I won't even ask him a question—I'll just listen to him, that's all—just listen!

TILDA. (*Almost inaudibly.*) Do as you please.

SAM. (*Snapping.*) What I please to do is finish the tree!—you want to help me? (*Silence. She is turned away from him.*) All right, I'll do it myself! (*As he proceeds with the decoration of the tree, she places herself in a position where she can watch an imaginary television set. She turns the selector dial, then the one for contrast. She sits back and watches impassively for a moment.*) What are you doing?

TILDA. Can't you see what I'm doing? I'm watching television.

SAM. What a horrible way to go. (*No comment from TILDA. She continues watching a moment, dislikes the program, dials another channel. This channel is disgusting.*)

TILDA. Yuch! (*She turns to another channel. This one gives her no displeasure.*)

SAM. What are you watching?

TILDA. (*Soberly.*) Yesterday you would have known.

SAM. Today I don't. What are you watching?

TILDA. The baseball game.

SAM. There's no baseball in February.

TILDA. (*It doesn't come too easily.*) There are no Christmas trees either. (*Dead stop. He comes down off the ladder. He stands between her and the television. He turns off the set.*)

SAM. (*Patiently.*) All right . . . let's say the worst happens. The Person comes in and tells me who Jesse is

and I remember something from back there. What difference can it make? If things were better than they are
here, why am I here? I've told you: *I've already made
the choice!*

TILDA. (*Quietly.*) We think we make choices, but we
don't. The choices make us.

SAM. Whatever I do, it's not my fault, is it?

TILDA. I didn't say it was your fault! I'm not blaming
you!

SAM. (*Hotly.*) Then what are you angry about?

TILDA. (*Bursting out.*) For that very reason!—there's
nobody to blame! I don't know a damn thing about
science but somewhere I learned about cause and effect!
If something makes you unhappy, there must be something to blame! But—there—is—nothing—to—blame!

SAM. That lets us off the hook, doesn't it?—we don't
have to blame ourselves, do we? Well, you're wrong
about that. We do make choices—and we are responsible
for them. And as between back there and you, Tilda—
I've chosen you! There isn't even a contest! Whatever
The Person tells me, whatever he has to offer, whatever I
make myself remember, it can only be second best!
(*Then, pulling himself back.*) As a matter of fact, I'm
quite sure that whatever he tells me will make me very
unhappy.

TILDA. . . . Then why do you want to hear it? (*It is
the crux of his confusion. The question gives him a bad
moment.*)

SAM. . . . I don't know. (*Seeing the tumult in him,
she doesn't push him too hard.*)

TILDA. Sammy . . . I lied to you.

SAM. About what?

TILDA. About what I can remember . . . I told you
there's nothing. But that's not true. I can remember . . .
myself. Just one glimpse of myself . . . very clearly—
right through the window. And if The Person gets you to
remember *your*self the way I do mine—oh Sammy, I don't

want you to have to do that! (*Shaken, she tries to pull herself together. Succeeding somewhat, she continues.*) I don't know where I was. I was crouching somewhere—it felt dark and damp—I think it was a cellar. How I got there—I don't know how—I didn't know the reason— except I wanted to be in total darkness. The light was too disturbing—it hurt me. Wherever there was daylight —the weakest ray of it—I couldn't bear to open my eyes. And even in the cellar, it wasn't dark enough. There was a light from a furnace . . . When I shut the furnace door I was still sure I could see it. So I tried to put it out— and I burned myself. Then, at last, it was out and I thought: it's dark now, I can keep my eyes open, it won't hurt me to keep my eyes open. But there was a crack somewhere—in the wall—and through it . . . a narrow white light . . . a knifeblade of light. I couldn't stand it. I tried to shut my eyes but I could see it, I could feel it cutting through my eyelids! Suddenly there was a flame in my head—it felt as if my brain was on fire and it was so unbearable that I—with my hands—with my fingernails—I tried to tear my eyes out of my head. I gouged at them—I could feel the pain and the blood— and still I couldn't shut the light out—I couldn't shut the light out—! (*There is a question whether she is able to manage herself without help. Acutely concerned for her,* SAM *takes a step toward her, but she raises her hand to prevent him; she is intent on managing herself without assistance. He stops. At last she is under her own control. She speaks quietly.*) That's all I remember. But it is conceivable to me that someday I may remember more. I think I want to. But I am certain that if I do remember more, it will turn out to be even more terrible. (*At last she looks at him.*) And if that could also be true of you, I beg you not to try too hard to bring it back. The pain's not in here, Sammy—it's out there. . . . This is the asylum from it.

SAM. Perhaps my memories might not be as painful as yours.

TILDA. (*With troubled reluctance.*) You haven't seen yourself remembering.

SAM. (*Hesitating . . . dreading.*) You mean it's . . . even worse than I think?

TILDA. . . . Yes. (*He stops. His dread is too deep for him to continue. At last:*)

SAM. When was the last time?

TILDA. Yesterday—before The Person came in.

SAM. No! I didn't hurt you, Tilda!—don't you bring that up again! I didn't hurt you!

TILDA. You could have.

SAM. No, Tilda!

TILDA. Not meaning to!—you could have! You could have hurt anybody!

SAM. (*Starting to lose control.*) Not you! I could never hurt you!

TILDA. Anybody!—whoever was near you!

SAM. No!—no!

TILDA. You started to remember something and you couldn't stand it! Whoever it was, you wanted to kill him!

SAM. (*On the run.*) No! You're making it up!—no!

TILDA. You *tried* to kill him! You struck at him again and again!

SAM. (*Starting to fall apart.*) I didn't, I didn't!

TILDA. You slashed at him! You made sounds like an animal!

SAM. (*An outcry.*) No!

TILDA. And it didn't matter who it was! Any second it might have been me!

SAM. No—no!

TILDA. It might have been somebody you *couldn't* remember!

SAM. (*He collapses now, to his knees.*) No! Then I won't remember anything! I won't remember, I won't! I'll never try to remember again! I'll never see The Person again—never! If he comes in, I'll lie down on the floor with my face down! I won't see him, I won't see anything, I won't see anything! (*Shaken to pieces; weep-*

ing.) Oh, hold me, hold me! (*She holds him close to her-self.*)

TILDA. Sammy—Sammy—

SAM. And if he comes in here, don't you look at him either! Don't give him a glance! If he makes you listen to him—if he tries to talk you out of this place— (*She fondles him, she mothers him.*)

TILDA. Sh. Sh. No, darling, no. Everything's going to be all right, everything will. Shhh. (*At last, being comforted, his sobbing subsides. She has helped him to lie down, his head in her lap. Now she wipes his eyes with the sleeve of her blouse. They are quite still. Then:*) Shall we pretend something?

SAM. (*In a small voice. Miserable.*) . . . No.

TILDA. It'll make you happy again.

SAM. I don't want to be anything now . . . not even happy. I just want to be . . . nothing. (*Quietly, out of the shadows,* THE PERSON *appears. For a while he watches them without their knowing it. Then* TILDA, *with a start, becomes aware of him. She whispers to* SAM.)

TILDA. Careful!

SAM. Why?

TILDA. Somebody's watching us.

SAM. No . . . nobody.

TILDA. Behind us.

SAM. (*He turns and sees* THE PERSON.) . . . Yes.

TILDA. What'll we do?

SAM. Get rid of him . . . make a fool of him.

TILDA. Yes—how?

SAM. Come on—we're going to dance. (*He holds his arms out. She goes into them with a squeal of delight.*)

TILDA. What a lovely idea! Did you send me a corsage?

SAM. (*As they dance.*) Yes—gardenias.

TILDA. With a sprig of forget-me-nots?

SAM. A small sprig, yes.

TILDA. Oh, it's lovely, thank you!—and it smells delicious.

SAM. The pin is sticking in my neck.

TILDA. I'm doing a waltz, what are you doing?

SAM. The polka. Or is that something you do with a beer barrel?

TILDA. You're thinking of the tarantella.

SAM. No, I'm not. That's a large hairy spider.

TILDA. I knew a spider once. He was waiting to lure a fly. Just waiting, waiting.

SAM. (*Quietly.*) Is he still waiting?

TILDA. (*Also quiet.*) Yes . . . I think so.

SAM. You're slowing down.

TILDA. (*Speeding up.*) No, I'm not, no I'm not!

SAM. He's talking.

TILDA. (*Sharply.*) Don't look at him!

SAM. I think it's you he wants to talk to.

TILDA. You're looking at him!

SAM. No I'm not!

TILDA. Then how would you know that?

SAM. Yes—it is you! He just said your name! (*Halt! She stops dancing.*)

TILDA. *How would you know that?* (*Silence.* SAM *and* TILDA *are separated, quite a distance. In the stillness* THE PERSON *moves down toward them. It is not immediately clear which of them he's heading for. Then we see that it is* TILDA. *He now turns his attention exclusively to her. As he opens his mouth and speaks to her, mouthing words we cannot hear,* SAM *interrupts.*)

SAM. Let her alone!

TILDA. Sammy— (THE PERSON *continues to speak.*)

SAM. I said let her alone!

TILDA. Don't worry about it, Sam—I can't hear a word he says! (THE PERSON *gestures for her to sit down.*)

SAM. Don't sit down, Tilda! You let her alone, I said! (*He grabs* THE PERSON *and turns him around.*)

TILDA. Sammy—!

SAM. You son of a bitch! (*He is about to do something violent when* TILDA *rushes between him and* THE PERSON.)

TILDA. Sammy—no—please! (*She succeeds in prevent-*

ing SAM. *The instant she has done so,* SAM *becomes aware of what he was on the verge of doing. He shakes his head like a dog shaking water off. He trembles. In that moment,* THE PERSON *again moves between* SAM *and* TILDA. *Now he gives his attention to* SAM. *With utmost solicitude he speaks to* SAM—*quietly but urgently. At last* SAM *looks outward, not at* THE PERSON, *not at* TILDA, *not at anyone.* THE PERSON *continues to speak.* TILDA *watches with growing apprehension. Now it seems to her that* SAM *is listening.*) Sam . . . don't listen! (*But* SAM *is listening. Now he even turns his head a little, directly to* THE PERSON. *The latter gestures to the same box* SAM *sat on yesterday when* THE PERSON *was here.* SAM *is confused: whether to sit or not.*)

TILDA. No, Sammy! Don't sit down! (THE PERSON *continues his quiet persuasion.* SAM *at last sits.* TILDA *is in a rout, not knowing what to do.*)

TILDA. Sammy—please—please don't listen! You—Person—stop talking to him! He can't help listening but you can help talking! Stop it! All right, I can talk as well as you can! Just as logically and just as persuasively! And if he listens to both of us, maybe he won't hear either of us, but there's a chance he'll hear me! There's entirely too much talking going on in the world! There's entirely too much of everything going on in the world! What we desperately need are large *inactivities!* We need great huge pockets of nothing! Places to hide in! Attics—cellars—crawl spaces! (*A note of desperation.*) Sammy, please don't listen! (*She resumes her prattling.*) If there's a choice of everybody paying attention to everybody and nobody paying attention to nobody—I'd choose nobody paying attention! That's neutral at least—and it's honest! That way we don't do violence to one another—we simply do not notice someone's there! And we— (*Again desperate.*) Sammy, don't listen! (*She hurries around to the other side so she can face* THE PERSON.) You can talk to him as much as you like but he won't listen to you! And if he does listen, he won't talk to you!—*he won't talk to you! (Abruptly* THE PERSON *stops talking.* TILDA *at first doesn't know why. Now, as she quickly changes her position, she sees the reason:* SAM *has started to speak. His mouth is moving, but she cannot hear the words—neither can we. She lets out a cry.)* No! Sammy—don't talk to him! Sammy—don't! I can't hear you! *(She cannot bear to look. She lets out a forlorn cry and turns away from them, she seeks a place to hide but cannot find one. She makes herself as small as she can. Meanwhile,* SAM *is talking, slowly, haltingly and altogether unheard by us. From her corner,* TILDA *makes herself look at them covertly, out of her misery. At last* SAM *stops speaking and is still. So is* THE PERSON. *The latter nods, rises and departs. The place is utterly silent. At last* SAM *turns to* TILDA. *He speaks aridly. Nothing he says comes easily to him.)*

SAM. You were right. He didn't answer any of the big questions. About God . . . or why people love each other . . . why they die . . . It all had to do with the breakfast dishes and locking doors at night and . . . thing like that . . . You were right about the other thing too. The name . . . Jesse. It's not a woman's' name. It's the name of a boy . . . a little boy . . . he's three-years old. He's my son. My wife's name is Harriet. Our breakfast dishes are white—not all white, there's a tiny border of blue flowers around the edges. And there's enough . . . enough . . . *(He has lost his way. It confuses, pains and finally enrages him.)* . . . enough murder to go around!— everyone can have a share! *(Angry at himself for the outburst, he pulls himself back to the calm.)* We live in a small house. A clapboard house—with white shutters. There's foundation planting on one side—I can't see the other sides very well. Jesse's room is blue—blue is for boys, pink is for girls. I have a car, I think. Yes, it's pale gray. It's hard starting in the winter time. Jesse can't say the word "yellow"—he says "lello." Harriet is worried that it may be a speech defect, but I'm sure it's not—I think he speaks very well for a three-year-old. And he

loves me very much. He waits for me to come home . . .
he always waits . . .

TILDA. (*Hardly a whisper; in pain.*) Stop it.

SAM. (*Compulsively.*) I teach in a high school somewhere. I don't know why—when there's so much trouble
in schools these days—I don't seem to have any trouble.
My students like me . . . they even say they like me.
History. I'm a teacher of History. (*Wryly.*) It was
strange teaching History when I wasn't remembering
. . . because History is memory . . . but if I can't remember. . . . (*An instant, then:*) I like teaching the
social sciences because I know exactly what's wrong:
everything. My students concur with that. And every day
we make things over . . . and over . . . and over. And
Harriet says, "Don't, Samuel—please don't. Leave things
as they are. Be happy. You have everything. A wife who
loves you and a child and a good home. Be happy . . .
with your life." (*Now comes his greatest hurdle: whether
to say this.*) There is nothing that she ever says that con-
vinces me . . . except that I love her.

TILDA. Please.

SAM. And I love Jesse.

TILDA. (*Trying to bury her head.*) If you don't stop
it . . . !

SAM. I'm not saying it to hurt you. It has nothing to
do with you. It's another world.

TILDA. You're going back to it.

SAM. No I'm not.

TILDA. Please.

SAM. I'm not.

TILDA. Don't lie to me. Didn't I see you listening to
The Person? Didn't I see you talking to him?

SAM. Tilda—

TILDA. Didn't I?—didn't I?

SAM. Yes.

TILDA. (*Ejecting it.*) You're a crud! You're a dirty
rotten crud!

SAM. Tilda, stop it!

TILDA. It doesn't occur to you it was a betrayal! That doesn't occur to you, does it?

SAM. I couldn't help it, Tilda! I didn't know I was doing it! I was simply doing it. One minute I couldn't stand anything—and the next minute he was helping me!

TILDA. I would have helped you!—couldn't you let me help you?

SAM. Apparently I couldn't, Tilda. (*He says it with utter quiet and it forces quiet upon her. In this more controlled mood, she asks:*)

TILDA. What did he do for you?

SAM. He said I had to "carry over" . . . and he would help me to do it.

TILDA. Carry over? . . . what does that mean?

SAM. Live in one world instead of two.

TILDA. You mean . . . only in the other one.

SAM. No . . . both . . . I have to make them both into one.

TILDA. You mean I'm to be Harriet and Harriet's to be me?

SAM. Not exactly that.

TILDA. Exactly what, then?

SAM. (*Confused.*) I—don't know, Tilda. I don't understand it any better than you do—but—where we all fit together—

TILDA. I don't fit anywhere but here!—and neither do you!—you'll make yourself miserable anywhere else!

SAM. I didn't say I was going anywhere else, did I?

TILDA. You don't have to say it! I know it!

SAM. (*After a moment.*) . . . I'm only going to . . . another room. (*This is it: what she dreaded.*)

TILDA. . . . Another room?

SAM. Yes.

TILDA. . . . Here?

SAM. Yes.

TILDA. But . . . away from me.

SAM. Yes.

TILDA. That's because I'm—I think there is an expression for what I am—a bad influence.

SAM. I didn't say that—and he didn't.

TILDA. Well, I'm certainly not a good one, am I?

SAM. We . . . it's both of us . . . when we're together, we go on pretending.

TILDA. And that's bad, is it? (*Silence.*) Answer me, goddamn it! It's bad, isn't it? When we pretend, when we make things bearable by laughing, by playing games, by being happy—that's bad, isn't it? (*With sudden anger.*) You're thinking the way they do! If we find ways of escaping them, they don't like that! If we find little mouse holes we can crawl through, they plug them up! It's perfectly all right if they form a conspiracy to torture us, but the minute we conspire to make a little happiness for ourselves, the minute we put up the Christmas tree, they walk right through it to show us how insane we are! They smash it! . . . And now you're listening to them— you're ready to go into another room. What will you find there?

SAM. Harriet and my son. (*Since he has not spared her, she doesn't spare him:*)

TILDA. You've had them!—and you wound up in here! —with me!

SAM. . . . And I may again.

TILDA. Then what are you going out for?

SAM. I love them, Tilda.

TILDA. (*She takes the blow.*) Oh, that's the killer thing to say, my friend! You've got the killer tools all ready and waiting, haven't you? I thought—when was it?—a hundred years ago?—a month ago?—no, only a few minutes ago—you said you loved *me,* Samuel.

SAM. And I do.

TILDA. Wouldn't you say that's something of a lie?

SAM. Yes . . . it's pretend.

TILDA. (*Under her breath.*) Oh, Christ.

SAM. If we live here by pretend, everything we do is pretend, Tilda. And that's how I love you.

TILDA. (*An outcry.*) Stop, stop!

SAM. I'm sorry, but pretend does hurt.

TILDA. (*In a furious outburst.*) No, it's not pretend, it's real that hurts!—real! Go back there and love her— love her real! And you'll see that it hurts a hell of a lot more than pretend!

SAM. Yes . . . you may be right.

TILDA. And that's what you want!

SAM. It hasn't anything to do with what I want, Tilda. What I want is to live back there—or here—anywhere —and not be miserable. I used to want to be happy, but I'll just settle for not being miserable! It was almost possible in here—except I can't keep the outside world outside—it keeps coming in. And I can't do anything about it. I don't think I'll ever be able to do anything about it if I stay in here.

TILDA. And out there you'll be able to do something, won't you? You were so successful at it before.

SAM. It may be hell again, Tilda. I won't have Christmas whenever I want it. Sometimes when it's really Christmas, I won't have it. But maybe I'll be able to make a deal with myself: Give up some of the illusions and get rid of some of the terrors. That man in the alley . . . maybe he'll identify himself.

TILDA. That's quite a deal.

SAM. . . . Yes.

TILDA. All right—you go on. (*In deadly quiet.*) I hope your whole world turns real.

SAM. You don't say that like a benediction.

TILDA. No, it's a curse! I hope your whole world turns real!

SAM. Thank you.

TILDA. (*With a cry of remorse.*) Oh, Sammy, I take it back—I don't want you hurt!—if you go back there you'll get hurt! You'll make yourself miserable! You'll kill yourself! Or worse!—you'll kill somebody else!

SAM. That's what I'm doing here!

TILDA. Whoever you're killing here isn't real—it's all

pretend! It's death today and life again tomorrow! It's all beginnings—every day is a second chance! You can kill a hundred people and you don't kill anybody!

SAM. *I kill me!* You're wrong about this place. You think everything can go on in the pretend world without hurting. I tell you it hurts more than when it's real—because there's no limit to it. Before The Person came in yesterday, I murdered a man. He wasn't real, he didn't exist, but I murdered him. I don't know who he was—I couldn't see his face. That made him everybody! It made him you. It made him Harriet. It made him my son Jesse. And it made him me! Is it any more bearable because I'm pretending? No, I'm still killing everybody I love—and I'm killing myself! And I'll go on doing it until I see the face of the person I'm murdering! I've got to see his face!

TILDA. That's what The Person told you!

SAM. No, that's what I told him!

TILDA. I don't believe it! It doesn't sound like your talk—it sounds like theirs! All made up—and logical and reasonable! Sammy, don't listen to their reasonable reasons! That's how they trick you into going back! They make you believe reason is the only reason! Reason is the worst reason—it's the worst, the worst, the worst! (*She has lost track. Moment by moment, she is deranging herself. He speaks quietly to her.*)

SAM. Tilda, he said he was going to make arrangements and he was coming back and—

TILDA. (*An outcry.*) No! I won't let you go!

SAM. Tilda, listen to me—

TILDA. I won't let you go! (*Savagely.*) Just play ball, that's all—play ball!

SAM. Tilda—

TILDA. (*Wild now—she is the umpire again.*) Play ball!

SAM. Tilda, stop it!

TILDA. Strike! Strike one!

SAM. Tilda—please—honey—

TILDA. Don't come near me, just play ball! Play ball, Goddamn it! (*Unleashed now.*) Or watch television—do the Christmas tree—!

SAM. Tilda—sweetheart—Tilda!

TILDA. You can't hurt me! You don't exist! I made you up! You're like Tankee and The Twins! I made you up! You're in the window and you're a reflection of nothing!—you don't exist!

SAM. Tilda!

TILDA. You don't exist! Take your hands away!

SAM. Stop it!

TILDA. If you hit me, I'll hit you right back! (*Now she starts to hit him. It is the most harrowing of "pretends." She strikes at the air, at his imaginary form. Each of her blows is accompained by an anguished outcry— she is torturing herself.*)

SAM. (*As she beats his imaginary self.*) Stop it! Tilda— please—please stop it! You're not hitting me, Tilda, you're hitting the air, you're hitting nothing! You're not hurting me—you're hurting yourself! Stop it! Stop it— please—please! (*He cannot bear seeing her torment. He is weeping for her. But she continues beating at the air, making monstrous noises, part shriek, part vomit, until she is totally spent. Now, only the low sound of her sobbing, as The Person re-enters. He beckons for SAM to come. SAM hesitates. In that moment, TILDA comes only partially to herself.*)

TILDA. (*A scream—to The Person.*) No—go away— you can't have him—go away! (THE PERSON *beckons to* SAM *again, this time a bit more peremptorily.*)

SAM. (*Quietly.*) I love you, Tilda. (*Quickly, he follows* THE PERSON. *The instant he is gone:*)

TILDA. No!—come back! Sammeeeee! (*Silence now. She looks around. She must find someone. She calls:*) Tankee! (*She waits. She searches the emptiness.*) Tankeeeee! . . . Taaaankee. (*Void. Nobody. She is terrified. She is unutterably lonely.*) Somebody . . . (*Nothing. The stillness is as profound as death. Slowly, very slowly, not knowing what she is doing, she sits down. Then a sound comes out of her, unnatural and unreal, like the lonely crying of a manufactured doll.*) Mama! (*Stillness.*) Ma-ma! (*Stillness.*) Ma-ma! (*Stillness. She is still. She is catatonically still. The lights go to black.*)

CURTAIN

BARBRA'S WEDDING
Daniel Stern

The Schiffs are the only non-celebrities in their Malibu neighborhood; in fact, their shabby house is next to Barbra Streisand's mansion. As the play opens, Jerry is in a frenzy over the media circus surrounding Barbra's 1998 wedding. An out-of-work actor with one small TV role on his résumé, he resents his obscurity—he wasn't even invited to the wedding! He rages against Streisand, Hollywood, the media, his wife and everything else. His wife tries to leave him—but Schwartzennegger's Humvee is blocking the driveway. This anti-show business comedy by a Hollywood insider is a hilarious send-up with a happy ending. "A ... play in the mold of Elaine May's comedies about people brought near to madness by the quirks of life."—*New York Post*. 1 m., 1 f. (#4901)

DIRTY BLONDE
Claudia Shear
Original score by Bob Stillman

A bawdy New York hit with dream roles, *Dirty Blonde* is "hands down the best new American play of the season....Take off your hats, boys, Mae West is back on Broadway ... in a compact Rolls Royce of a vehicle. This is no evening of mere impersonation.... *Dirty Blonde* is a multi-layered study of the nature of stardom ... [that] finds the enduring substance in the smoke and mirrors of one actress's stardom, allowing Mae West to shock and delight once again."—*The New York Times*. Vocal Score available. 2 m., 1 f. (#6929)

THE BASIC CATALOGUE OF PLAYS AND MUSICALS
online at www.samuelfrench.com

TALKING HEADS 1 & 2
Alan Bennett

Six of these monologues by the inventive author of *Beyond the Fringe* and *The Madness of George III* were revived Off Broadway with a stellar cast that included Lynn Redgrave: *The Hand of God, A Lady of Letters* and *Bed Among the Lentils* on one night; *Her Big Chance, A Chip in the Sugar* and *Miss Fozzard Finds Her Feet* the next evening. Also in the two volumes: *A Cream Cracker Under the Settee, Soldiering On* and *The Outside Dog*. "Diamond-cut ... classics.... Mr. Bennett's work is too seldom seen on these shores."—*The New York Times.* "Each character has his or her own verbal music.... *Talking Heads* has brought great joy to this ... season."—*New York Daily News.* (#9935)

SECOND LADY
M. Kilburg Reedy

Originally seen Off Broadway starring Judith Ivey, this remarkable play has been applauded in theatres nationally and internationally. Ideal for an actress in her forties or fifties, *Second Lady* is a powerful 70-minute performance piece about a fictional political wife. She has mislaid her prepared remarks and must draw on personal experiences to fulfill a speaking engagement. Her recollections bring her face to face with the truth about her life and marriage. "A searing and soaring experience."—*Hollywood Reporter.* Published with *Astronaut* and *Fairytale Romance* in *Second Lady and Other Ladies.* (#20941)

For more Broadway and Off-Broadway hits, see
THE BASIC CATALOGUE OF PLAYS AND MUSICALS
online at www.samuelfrench.com

Blue

A PLAY BY
Charles Randolph-Wright

MUSIC BY
Nona Hendrix

LYRICS BY
Nona Hendryx and Charles Randolph-Wright

Using music as an integral part of the storytelling, Blue spans nearly twenty years in the life of the affluent African-American Clark family in rural South Carolina. Events are seen through the eyes of the eldest son Reuben, who evolves from a preteen trumpet player into an adult artist. His mother, a relentlessly chic matriarch with dark secrets who is out of place in the her provincial surroundings, holds court at family gatherings. She lays out grandiose plans for her two sons while the mesmerizing music of sexy jazz singer Blue Williams adds a unique dimension. Meanwhile, her husband runs a profitable funeral home, grandmother offers unsolicited advice and Ruben's brother runs with the girls. This humorous family portrait abounds with tenderness, acceptance and the search for unconditional love while introducing audiences to an African-American family the likes of which is seldom portrayed on stage or screen.

THE BASIC CATALOGUE OF PLAYS AND MUSICALS
online at www.samuelfrench.com

The Twilight of the Golds
JONATHAN TOLINS

"Funny, thoughtful, and most eerily topical."
San Francisco Chronicle

"A haunting play of ideas crucial to the way we live."
Rex Reed

"An entertaining theatrical tempest."
Washington Times

"A rich, intelligent, articulate piece of work."
Los Angeles Times

If your parents knew everything about your before you were born, would you be here? That is the question posed in this comic drama. All is well when Suzanne Gold and her close New York family discover that she is pregnant, until a new prenatal test reveals that the baby will most likely be homosexual. 3 m., 2 f. (#22254)

Lebensraum
ISRAEL HOROWITZ

"Powerful and touching."
The New York Times

Using a cast of three to play forty sharply drawn characters, this bold work of penetrating intelligence is based on the fanciful, explosive idea that a German Chancellor might, as an act of redemption, invite six million Jews to Germany with a promise of citizenship and jobs. A resulting scenario unfolds that explores the effects of this policy. 2 m., 1 f.

**Send for your copy of the Samuel French
BASIC CATALOGUE OF PLAYS AND MUSICALS**